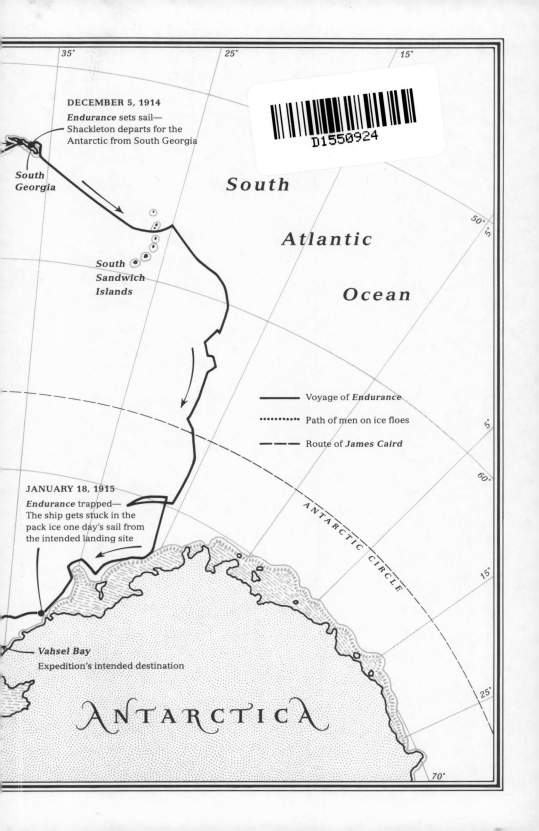

35°   25°   15°

DECEMBER 5, 1914
Endurance sets sail—
Shackleton departs for the
Antarctic from South Georgia

*South
Georgia*

D1550924

South

50°
5′

*South
Sandwich
Islands*

A t l a n t i c

5′

———— Voyage of *Endurance*

•••••••••• Path of men on ice floes

– – – – Route of *James Caird*

60°

JANUARY 18, 1915
Endurance trapped—
The ship gets stuck in the
pack ice one day's sail from
the intended landing site

ANTARCTIC CIRCLE

15°

Vahsel Bay
Expedition's intended destination

25°

$\mathcal{A}$NTARCTIC$\mathcal{A}$

70°

SHACKLETON'S WAY

SIR ERNEST SHACKLETON, 1874–1922

SHACKLETON'S WAY

Leadership Lessons from the
Great Antarctic Explorer

MARGOT MORRELL
STEPHANIE CAPPARELL

with a preface by
The Honorable Alexandra Shackleton

To Barney,

thank you for
your advice and support.

Stephanie
1-22-01

VIKING

VIKING
Published by the Penguin Group
Penguin Putnam Inc., 375 Hudson Street,
New York, New York 10014, U.S.A.
Penguin Books Ltd, 27 Wrights Lane,
London W8 5TZ, England
Penguin Books Australia Ltd, Ringwood,
Victoria, Australia
Penguin Books Canada Ltd, 10 Alcorn Avenue,
Toronto, Ontario, Canada M4V 3B2
Penguin Books (N.Z.) Ltd, 182–190 Wairau Road,
Auckland 10, New Zealand

Penguin Books Ltd, Registered Offices:
Harmondsworth, Middlesex, England

First published in 2001 by Viking Penguin,
a member of Penguin Putnam Inc.

1   3   5   7   9   10   8   6   4   2

Grateful acknowledgment is made for permission to reprint excerpts from the following copy-righted works:
    Diary of Thomas Orde-Lees. By permission of Dartmouth College Library, Hanover, New Hampshire.
    Diaries of Thomas Orde-Lees and Harry McNish. By permission of Alexander Turnbull Library, Wellington, New Zealand.
    V: A Novel by Thomas Pynchon. Copyright © 1961, 1963 by Thomas Pynchon. Reprinted by permission of HarperCollins Publishers, Inc.
    Papers in the collection of the Scott Polar Research Institute. By permission of Scott Polar Research Institute, University of Cambridge, Cambridge, England.
    Memoir of Frank Wild. By permission of the Mitchell Library, State Library of New South Wales, Sydney, Australia.

LIBRARY OF CONGRESS CATALOGING-IN-PUBLICATION DATA

Morrell, Margot.
    Shackleton's way : leadership lessons from the great Antarctic explorer / Margot Morrell and Stephanie Capparell ; with a preface by Alexandra Shackleton.
        p. cm.
    ISBN 0-670-89196-7
    1. Leadership. 2. Shackleton, Ernest Henry, 1874–1922. 3. Strategic planning. 4. Survival skills. 5. Teams in the workplace. 6. Explorers—Antarctica. I. Capparell, Stephanie. II. Title.

HD57.7.M668 2000   00-034982

This book is printed on acid-free paper. ∞

Printed in the United States of America
Set in Versailles
Designed by Carla Bolte

FOR

ALISON AND JEANNIE

&

ROZ, NEVA, AND SUSAN

OUR SISTERS, OUR BEST FRIENDS

You wait. Everyone has an Antarctic.

—Thomas Pynchon, *V.*

PREFACE

AS A CHILD, I DO NOT REMEMBER ANYONE SITTING ME DOWN AND telling me about my grandfather, Ernest Shackleton. Somehow, I seem always to have known that he was a great Antarctic explorer. I knew that he had died in 1922, at age forty-seven, whilst leading his third expedition and that my father, Edward, had been ten years old at the time. I was proud of my grandfather but his world seemed very remote from mine.

That sense of distance changed in 1991 when I spent a month in the Antarctic on board the HMS *Endurance*, the Royal Navy's ice-patrol vessel, named after my grandfather's most famous ship. "By Endurance We Conquer" is the Shackleton family motto. That trip was for me full of moments that resonated from my grandfather's time. It was a poignant and wonderful experience. Indeed, most people never quite recover from their first visit to Antarctica. It is an extraordinary place. I remember meeting the captain of the new *Endurance* when he had just returned from his first deployment to the South, where his ship had gone deep into the Weddell Sea. He had the shell-shocked expression of anyone with a soul when first encountering Antarctica. He told me he was unable to tear himself away from the bridge as he approached the continent, such were the sights unfolding before his eyes. I understood.

Three years later, the Royal Navy took me to visit my grandfather's grave at Grytviken, a whaling station abandoned on the island of South Georgia. At another station nearby, Stromness, I was to unveil a plaque commemorating the arrival of Ernest Shackleton and his companions on May 20, 1916, after their epic boat journey from Elephant Island and their trek over the uncharted, mountainous interior of South Georgia. As the ship approached Cumberland East Bay, I was seeing colors that my grandfather would have seen: the blue of the mighty Nordenskjold Glacier and the surprising gentle green of the neighboring slopes.

I was standing on the bridge of a ship that would have astonished my grandfather, who had begun his maritime career on board sailing vessels. The HMS *Norfolk* was equipped with state-of-the-art sensors and communication equipment and carried a Lynx helicopter. The ship's first lieutenant and I packed ourselves into orange survival suits and were flown ashore over the magnificent Neumayer Glacier. All was calm, although flying here is often bedeviled by fierce katabatic winds gusting up to eighty knots and creating "drainage," which drags an aircraft downward. We landed at King Edward Point, were welcomed by the garrison, and set off up the path toward the graveyard. A small but determined fur seal blocked our way. He looked at me then looked at the first lieutenant, as if he could not decide which one of us he hated more. Whilst he was coming to a decision, we hastily split up and went around him to the safety of the fenced graveyard.

Grandfather's grave lies at the far end, beneath a magnificent backdrop of mountains. The words engraved on the simple granite headstone read: *To the Dear Memory of Sir Ernest Shackleton, Explorer, Born 15 February 1874, Entered Life Eternal 5 January 1922.* Standing there, I felt huge regret that so many years separated our lives.

The next day, the *Norfolk* anchored in Stromness Bay, and the captain and I were flown ashore. I made a short speech at the whaling station and the plaque was unveiled outside the manager's

Villa. It is a handsome plaque, decorated with a profile of Shackleton, a drawing of the *James Caird,* and the story of the *Endurance* expedition. It was then time to go. As the *Norfolk* left South Georgia's spectacular coastline behind, I felt closer to my grandfather than ever before. South Georgia had witnessed his greatest achievement: turning disaster into triumph. It is right that he lies here.

Recently, there has been a great upsurge in interest in Sir Ernest Shackleton, of which this book is a distinguished example. I first met Margot Morrell in 1997, at the end of her thirteen years of impressive research on Shackleton's leadership qualities. Stephanie Capparell is a business journalist who helped fuel the renewal of interest in Shackleton with her 1998 article in *The Wall Street Journal.* Their conclusions on the lessons that business can learn from Ernest Shackleton's leadership are an innovative and excellent contribution to this growing body of literature.

As for me, the grandfather I never knew is no longer remote.

Alexandra Shackleton
London

CONTENTS

INTRODUCTION 1

Shackleton resonates with executives in today's business world. His people-centered approach to leadership can be a guide for anyone in a position of authority. Some of today's leaders are successfully applying Shackleton's methods to their own work situations.

1/THE PATH TO LEADERSHIP 15

The values Shackleton learned from his family helped form his uniquely progressive leadership style. He worked his way into the forefront of a new field. He turned bad experiences into valuable work lessons. He insisted on respectful competition in a business climate that often demanded cooperation.

U.S. Secretary of the Navy Richard Danzig sees Shackleton's broad cultural interests as a main ingredient of thoughtful leadership.

2/HIRING AN OUTSTANDING CREW 51

Shackleton built a crew around a core of experienced workers. He conducted unconventional interviews to find unique talent. His second in command was his most important hire. He looked for optimism and cheerfulness in the people he hired. He gave his staff the best compensation and equipment he could afford.

James Cramer credits Shackleton's optimistic example with saving his hedge fund and TheStreet.com from an early demise.

6/FORMING TEAMS FOR TOUGH ASSIGNMENTS 157

Shackleton balanced talent and expertise in each team. He ensured all his groups were keeping pace. He remained visible and vigilant. He shored up the weakest links. He got teams to help each other.

Apollo 13 commander James Lovell sees similarities in how Shackleton and he led their crews through crises.

7/OVERCOMING OBSTACLES TO REACH A GOAL 181

Shackleton took responsibility for getting the whole job done. Even "Old Cautious" sometimes took big risks. He found the inspiration to continue. He kept sight of the big picture. He stepped outside his work to help others.

Jaguar's retired chief of North American operations, Mike Dale, used Shackleton's story to spur his sales crew to new heights.

8/LEAVING A LEGACY 205

Shackleton's leadership had a lifelong impact on his crew. His appeal spans generations. He made lasting contributions to leadership. His influence on a pioneer project in space. Using his example to promote social change. How we view Shackleton's success today.

SHACKLETON'S WAY

SUCCESSFUL FAILURE

The *Endurance* expedition to the Antarctic (1914–1916), ultimately fell far short of its goal, but it would become a legendary success for the leader, Ernest Shackleton, who got every one of his men safely home after their ship sank in a remote, frozen sea. He did it by using leadership skills honed over more than two decades. His brilliant survival strategy seems particularly relevant to the high-risk, entrepreneurial spirit that characterizes business today.

First Row, left to right: Clark, Wordie, Macklin, Marston, McIlroy. Second Row: Cheetam, Crean, Hussey, Greenstreet, Shackleton, Gooch (a friend, seated), Rickinson, Hurley. Third Row: McNeish, James, Wild, Worsley, Hudson, How, Green. Last Row (center): Holness, Bakewell. Not pictured: Orde-Lees, Kerr, McCarthy, McLeod, Vincent, Blackborow, Stephenson.

INTRODUCTION

HE HAS BEEN CALLED "THE GREATEST LEADER THAT EVER CAME on God's earth, bar none," yet he never led a group larger than twenty-seven, he failed to reach nearly every goal he ever set, and, until recently, he had been little remembered after his death. But once you learn the story of Sir Ernest Shackleton and his remarkable Antarctic expedition of 1914–1916 you'll come to agree with the effusive praise of those under his command. He is a model of great leadership and, in particular, a master of guidance in crisis.

That's because Shackleton failed only at the improbable; he succeeded at the unimaginable. "I love the fight and when things [are] easy, I hate it," he once wrote to his wife, Emily. He failed to reach the South Pole in 1902 when he was part of a three-man Farthest South team on the *Discovery* expedition of the renowned explorer Robert F. Scott. But the men turned back only after walking their scurvy-ravaged bodies to within 460 miles of the Pole in a terrifying cold experienced only by a handful of human beings at that time. Six years later, commanding his own expedition, Shackleton was forced to turn back a heartbreaking 97 miles short of the Pole, but only after realizing it would be certain death by starvation had his team continued. He was forgiven that failure in light of the greatness of the effort; he was knighted by King Edward VII and honored as a hero throughout the world.

His greatest failure was his 1914–1916 *Endurance* expedition. He lost his ship before even touching Antarctica. But he reached a new pinnacle in leadership when he successfully led all the members of his crew to safety after a harrowing two-year fight for their lives.

It is a tale so amazing you'll wonder why the *Endurance* saga hasn't become a part of every school-age child's reading. If Shackleton's expeditions ultimately were all disappointments to him for falling short of their goals, he made plenty of grand achievements to his credit along the way. As a member of the *Discovery* team, Shackleton was among the first to attempt to reach the South Pole, or even to venture inland from the Antarctic Coast. He was the first to discover vegetation on a remote Antarctic island. His *Nimrod* expedition located the Magnetic South Pole, invaluable for navigational charts. He was the first to find coal in the Antarctic, altering how scientists saw the makeup and the origins of the continent. He pioneered innovations in exploration packing, clothing, diet, transport, and equipment.

Sir Ernest set out at age forty on an independent voyage to make what he considered the last great expedition left on earth: an eighteen-hundred-mile crossing of the Antarctic on foot. The expedition ship, named the *Endurance* after the Shackleton family motto *Fortitudine Vincimus*, "By Endurance We Conquer," set sail in August 1914 at the dawn of World War I and made its way to Buenos Aires, to South Georgia island, and eventually to the Antarctic Circle, where it plowed through one thousand miles of ice-encrusted waters. Just one day's sail from its destination in Vahsel Bay on the Antarctic coast, the ship got stuck "like an almond in a chocolate bar" as it was later described, in the polar ice of the Weddell Sea.

The men were stranded on an ice floe more than twelve hundred miles from the farthest outposts of civilization. Whenever it seemed the situation couldn't possibly get worse, it did. The pack ice precariously dragged the ship north for ten months. Then, the *Endurance* was crushed and the men were forced to camp on the ice. They watched in horror one month later as their vessel sank to the bottom of the sea. No one knew anything had happened to them. All they had to rely on were three rickety lifeboats salvaged from the ship. Shackleton allowed each crew member to carry only a few items necessary for survival. The first things tossed: gold coins and a Bible; saved were personal diaries and a banjo.

When the weather was its most brutal, the men endured temperatures that were so low they could hear the water freeze. The bitter cold froze their garments solid and burned their hands and feet. They slept in tents so flimsy they could see the moon through them. They spent nearly four months in the frigid darkness of the long polar night. When the Antarctic summer finally brought warmer temperatures and the promise of some relief, the men awoke every morning in cold puddles of water as their body heat melted the icy floor of their tents. They subsisted on a diet of mostly penguin, seal, and sometimes dog, fare that left them feeling weak and blubbery.

The New Zealand explorer Sir Edmund Hillary, writing in 1976 about the *Endurance* expedition, sympathized with their suffering: "Danger is one thing, but danger plus extreme discomfort for long periods is quite another. Most people can put up with a bit of danger—it adds something to the challenge—but no one likes discomfort."

Eventually, when the ice began shattering beneath them, the men took to their three small lifeboats. After more than four months of mind-numbing boredom, they suddenly were pitched into an intense battle for survival that brought them to the limits of human capabilities. They fought the sea for nearly a week, making their way to land. They were cold, hungry, exhausted, and so thirsty their tongues swelled in their mouths. When they finally reached Elephant Island, they found it a stinking, guano-covered spit of land constantly ravaged by storms. Most of the crew spent the last months of their ordeal huddled under two overturned lifeboats.

In the end, Shackleton took five men and sailed eight hundred miles in a lifeboat over tumultuous seas to reach the inhabited island of South Georgia in the remote South Atlantic. When by some miracle they made their destination, they found they had to cross a nearly impassable frozen mountain range to reach civilization: a whaling station. The whalers, who had seen so much in their own hard lives, were in awe of the invincibility of the men, horribly ravaged by the elements. Immediately, Shackleton turned around and led an effort to rescue the rest of the crew on Elephant Island. Amazingly, every single one had survived.

Credit Shackleton.

According to Napoleon, "a leader is a dealer in hope." Shackleton knew how to keep hope in plentiful supply—during the 1907–1909 *Nimrod* expedition to the Pole when death was nearer to the men than their waiting ship, and during the long hardship of the *Endurance* expedition. When it was preposterous to think they could get out alive, he convinced his men that only a fool would say they wouldn't. "We were in a mess, and the Boss was the man who could get us out. It is a measure of his leadership that this seemed almost axiomatic," said Reginald W. James, physicist on the *Endurance*.

"The Boss," as his men called him, built success on a foundation of camaraderie, loyalty, responsibility, determination, and—above all—optimism. Early polar exploration is full of haunting tales of the demise of men who didn't have the good fortune to be under the charge of a man such as Shackleton. They suffered horrible deaths from accidents, starvation, exposure, and disease; teetered on the brink of insanity; were driven to suicide; and were pushed to mutiny, murder, and even cannibalism.

The 1912 Antarctic expedition of Australian explorer Douglas Mawson ended in disaster. He lost his two companions—one to an accident and one to starvation—and was himself so stricken with scurvy he had to tie his soles back onto his feet after they had fallen off. The first American attempt to reach the North Pole, the *Polaris* expedition of 1871, was so fraught with dissention that the captain, Charles F. Hall, ended up being poisoned by his men. The ship subsequently descended further into chaos fed by lax discipline, drunkenness, and mental anguish. In the 1890s, some crew members of Admiral Robert E. Peary's voyages accused him of treating his men with "intolerant brutality" and blamed him for one, perhaps two, suicides. Another of America's Arctic explorers, Aldolphus Greely, lost nineteen of his twenty-five men to starvation and was forced to defend himself against accusations of cannibalism. Even the Ross Sea party, the other half of Shackleton's *Endurance* expedition assigned to lay depots on Antarctica for the crossing, lost three men: one to scurvy and two to a senseless accident.

Read what Dr. Frederick Cook, a crew member of the *Belgica*, the Belgian expedition to Antarctica, wrote in his diary on June 19, 1898, three months after his ship had become stuck in the ice: "Most of us in the cabin have grown decidedly gray within two months, though few are over thirty. Our faces are drawn, and there is an absence of jest and cheer and hope in our makeup, which in itself is one of the saddest incidents of our existence."

Compare that passage to what an *Endurance* crew member, Frank Hurley, wrote on June 21, 1915, five months after his ship had become frozen in the pack ice: "The Billabong [cabin] has an atmosphere poetic. Macklin in his bunk is writing poetical verses, and I am doing the same. McIlroy is arranging a décolleté dancing rig, whilst Uncle Hussey is being beset by applicants to rehearse accompaniments on his banjo."

Some sixty years after the rescue, an interviewer asked *Endurance* first officer Lionel Greenstreet, "How did you survive when so many expeditions perished?" The old salt, then eighty-two, answered in one word: "Shackleton."

British explorer Apsley Cherry-Garrard best expressed the feelings of his fellow "Antarcticists," as he called them, when he explained: "For a joint scientific and geographical piece of organization, give me Scott; for a winter journey, give me Wilson; for a dash to the Pole and nothing else, Amundsen; and if I am in the devil of a hole and want to get out of it, give me Shackleton every time."

For all his courage and risk-taking bravado, Shackleton wasn't careless. He had witnessed some of the horrors of expedition work and decided the stated goals, however noble, were not worth such misery and carnage. "Better a live donkey than a dead lion," he told his wife after turning back from his Farthest South journey on the *Nimrod* expedition. For Shackleton, people came first. He always chose to live another day to conquer another, even bigger, goal.

Shackleton couldn't keep away from the Antarctic, although he vowed to himself and his family many times that he would give up exploration. He paid dearly for his obsession. Photos of Shackleton taken in 1921 on his last voyage, aboard the *Quest,* show a haggard man aged far beyond his forty-seven years. His face is every bit the sum of the strain of past voyages and the extraordinary effort it had taken to save the lives of his companions five years earlier.

Shackleton's *Endurance* rescue was little appreciated at the time. The resurfacing of the lost crew made headlines around the world, but the public wasn't very interested in men who survived self-inflicted pain while striving for personal glory. Europe was engulfed in World War I and people preferred to pay tribute to those who sacrificed their lives for the flag.

The war hero was replacing the explorer hero. "People think nothing of being killed nowadays; it's looked on as an honor," *Endurance* crewman Thomas Orde-Lees lamented after his rescue. "They call it the Roll of Honor now instead of the Casualty List."

Today, Antarctica looms large in the Western psyche. It is a symbol of the unattainable dream, of absolute isolation, of man's hardest battle against nature, and of the ultimate measure of a person's mental and physical capabilities. It represents the kind of test that, if you survive it at all, it is by the skin of your teeth— and you emerge a better person for it.

Yet the continent is so uniquely beautiful. Anyone who has been to "The Ice," as it is called, speaks of its majesty, its profound quiet, and the extraordinary colors hidden in its simple blue and white scheme. Early explorers, writing about their voyages, would pause in the middle of hair-raising tales to describe the landscape. Australian explorer Louis C. Bernacchi, the physicist on Scott's *Discovery* expedition, wrote: "At times clouds of ice-crystals thinly veiled the sun as in a glittering tenuous garment, reflecting its rays so that the whole arch of the heavens was traced with circles and lines of brilliant prismatic or white light."

Many who travel to the Antarctic find themselves drawn to it again and again. Some describe travel there as a kind of religious experience, and say it's as much about the inner journey as about the actual distance covered. Even armchair travelers get hooked on the endless human drama of polar exploration and become lifelong students and collectors of Antarctic history and lore. It is the one place in the world virtually untouched by civilization, and is likely to remain so, even as environmentalists struggle to preserve its pristine nature. In 1959, an international agreement was signed dedicating the continent to peace and science. It is a continent firmly identified with the twentieth century: from the first explorations inland in the early 1900s to the booming tourism trade and scientific studies at the close of the century.

It was only fitting that on the eve of the new millennium, the public would become possessed of the kind of admiration for Shackleton that he enjoyed at the peak of his career. Today, museum exhibits, coffee-table books, documentaries, Hollywood scripts, and reprints of early accounts of his expeditions retell the tales of the *Nimrod* and the *Endurance*. An appetite for adventure stories, a search for worthy heroes, a need to find new models of results-oriented leadership all help feed the resurgence of his popularity. Another reason that Shackleton seems a man for the present is that we've grown weary of the culture of victimization and despair and are searching for leaders who are survivors and optimists and are able to lead us into a new era.

If it's true that we love most those leaders we would like to be, it's no surprise that we embrace Shackleton. He was a gentleman, a poet, and an adventurer. Men wanted to be around him. Women wanted him, period. He was strong, persuasive, and charming and had a fondness for nights of carousing. Of course, he had his faults—and they were widely known. He could be ruthless in pursuing objectives and unforgiving of people who challenged his authority. He was often careless with money and chased get-rich-quick deals. He was also self-absorbed. His work took him away from his wife and three children for long periods, and when he was home his attention sometimes strayed to other women.

This frivolous side, however, belied a more serious, sensitive nature capable of remarkable feats of leadership still relevant today. Neal F. Lane, science adviser to President Clinton and former director of the National Science Foundation, held up the example of Shackleton in a May 1995 commencement address at Michigan State University. "It is only by building a sense of teamwork and community—just as Shackleton and his crew did eighty years ago—that we can overcome the unexpected detours and hurdles we encounter on our own journeys, and gain the satisfaction that ought to derive from such achievements," he said. "Those organizations—be they businesses, schools, colleges and universities, government agencies—that prepare themselves for the unexpected and help to build a sense of community will, in my opinion, become the leaders in the twenty-first century. The same is true for each of us as individuals."

Shackleton faced many of the same problems encountered by managers today: bringing a diverse group together to work toward a common goal; handling the constant naysayer; bucking up the perpetual worrier; keeping the disgruntled from poisoning the atmosphere; battling boredom and fatigue; bringing order and success to a chaotic environment; working with limited resources.

He embodied the attributes of the best business leaders: those who have adroitly adapted to an accelerating revolution in the workplace. The principles of democracy that changed the map of the world in the late twentieth century have finally trickled down to the workplace. Hierarchies are being flattened and formalities abandoned. Even the highest-ranking bosses are rejecting many of the perks and trappings of the privileged taskmaster. They want success, but they also want to make a contribution to their fields and to their communities.

Employees, for their part, are better educated, better traveled, more ambitious, and worldlier than ever before. They resent being managed and driven; they want to be inspired and led. They expect to have intelligent exchanges with their bosses and to help guide the direction of their companies. They also have professional goals and personal interests beyond their current jobs. Best of all, the office is now one of the most diverse segments of society. Women and minorities are gaining more power in the workplace and are making changes in office culture.

A huge generational shift is also transforming the corporate world. Baby boomers are coming to power. Many of them never expected to become businesspeople sitting behind a desk. They understand Shackleton's discomfort with authoritarian roles and his personal restlessness. They reject many of the leadership and organizational models of the past: power hierarchies, the military, even the production line. *The Wall Street Journal* reported in April 1999 that when the head of a major clothing-store chain launched a management-training campaign in which retailing competition was compared to war, managers protested and some quit in anger. Indeed, the military now looks to the corporate world for a better method of managing personnel.

The most profound change, however, has been the leap from the bricks-and-mortar business world into cyberspace. Young, Internet-

savvy entrepreneurs are assuming management positions alongside veteran corporate leaders. Their investors ignored traditional
measures of success to explore new ventures. Is it any wonder that
Shackleton's voyage into the unknown is again capturing the public's imagination? Shackleton had to leave behind his wooden
barkentine, one of the last of its kind, to achieve a different sort of
triumph in a vast, open landscape. He wasn't very good at making
money but he opened doors to new worlds and brilliantly led
people through them. The tables have turned again, and the
pathfinder is reclaiming his place ahead of the war hero.

All these changes demand new leadership skills. Shackleton-
style leadership. Shackleton's strategy is the antithesis of the old
command-and-control models. His brand of leadership instead
values flexibility, teamwork, and individual triumph. It brings back
some of the gentlemanliness and decorum of the past, but without
the hidden agenda of an exclusionary inner circle. It's business
with a human face.

In matters of leadership, the most reliable sources are the ones
who are led, so the authors mainly studied the writings of men
who knew Shackleton personally for their analysis of Shackleton's
prowess. The diaries of the *Endurance* crewmen proved invaluable, particularly one kept by Thomas Orde-Lees, who was interested in leadership issues. Shackleton's generation, like our own,
was preoccupied with finding the secrets of good leaders and several of Shackleton's contemporaries wrote portraits of him in this
vein. The authors also consulted Shackleton's own writings as well
as research materials gathered by his family and other Shackleton
scholars. Shackleton's diaries and two autobiographical books,
however, fail to reveal the logic behind his strategy.

The myths that have been built around Shackleton imply he possessed superhuman qualities; but if you take a close look at his
story, as this book does, you will see the best qualities of his leadership are eminently learnable. Shackleton was an average person;
he taught himself how to be an exceptional one. He rose above his

peers and earned the unfailing loyalty of his men. His story is, in its essence, an inspirational tale about unleashing strengths in individuals that they never knew they had in order to achieve goals— from the small to the miraculous.

Shackleton's Way is a handbook for the new generation of leaders. It guides those who accept the new workplace sensibilities but are baffled by how to translate them into policy. Readers will learn how to develop and unify a staff despite varying backgrounds and abilities, how to organize into successful teams, and how to make individual workers feel appreciated and inspired. The book also demonstrates how to handle crises, particularly how to break bad news, to bolster morale, and to quickly change course in the face of the unexpected. Shackleton's example also shows the importance of injecting humor and fun into work, how to bond with a staff without losing status as the boss, and when to nurture.

The book details Shackleton's professional life, highlighting significant lessons gleaned from his work. It then shows how these lessons have been applied in today's world by businesspeople and other leaders who didn't have to go to the ends of the earth to find the *Endurance* spirit. The stories include, among others, how James Cramer of TheStreet.com credits the explorer's story with pushing him to achieve success when others told him to give up his fledgling business. Jeremy Larken of OCTO Ltd. in Chester, England, has adapted Shackleton's survival strategies to the management of modern-day business disasters. Mike Dale, former president of Jaguar North America, used the Shackleton story to help fire up his dealers and push them to new heights in sales. Harvard Business School graduate Luke O'Neill founded an expedition-based, nontraditional high school that is helping students achieve by building on Shackleton's philosophy of reaching beyond expectations. Secretary of the Navy Richard Danzig regards Shackleton as a model for treating servicemen as deserving professionals.

Anyone can benefit from these lessons: a teacher, a parent, a leader of a community organization, as well as the corporate manager. Shackleton's wisdom is by no means simple or obvious. Much of it is counterintuitive, especially for those schooled in more conventional management tactics. Shackleton served tea in bed to the ship's crybaby, flattered the egomaniacs, and kept close to him the most abrasive personalities. Often, he made great personal sacrifices. Sometimes he led by not leading at all.

R. W. Richards, a scientist on the Ross Sea party of the ill-fated expedition, said simply, "Shackleton, with all his faults, was a great man, or should I say, a great leader of men."

Shackleton made his men want to follow him; he did not force them to do so. In the process, he changed the way his crewmen saw themselves and the world. His work continued to inspire them for as long as they lived, and to inspire others around the world long after that. There is no greater tribute to a leader. His tools were humor, generosity, intelligence, strength, and compassion.

That's Shackleton's Way.

- "Courage and willpower can make miracles. I know of no better example than what that man has accomplished." —Roald Amundsen, Norwegian explorer and discoverer of the South Pole

- "He had a quick brain, and he could visualize things ahead, and as far as he could he safeguarded any eventuality that was likely to occur." —Lionel Greenstreet, first officer, *Endurance*

- "Shackleton: an attractive and interesting personality . . . a most cheerful person . . . born optimist and overflowed with energy." —Sir Douglas Mawson, Australian explorer

- "He was so young at heart that he appeared to be younger than any of us." —James A. McIlroy, surgeon on *Endurance* and *Quest*

- "His method of discipline was very fair. He did not believe in unnecessary discipline." —William Bakewell, seaman, *Endurance*

- "I always found him rising to his best and inspiring confidence when things were at their blackest." —Frank Hurley, photographer, *Endurance*

- "I do not think there is any doubt that we all owe our lives to his leadership and his power of making a loyal and coherent party out of rather diverse elements." —Reginald W. James, physicist, *Endurance*

- "No matter what turns up, he is always ready to alter his plans and make fresh ones, and in the meantime laughs, jokes, and enjoys a joke with anyone, and in this way keeps everyone's spirits up." —Frank Worsley, captain, *Endurance*

- "He was a tower of strength and endurance, and he never panicked in any emergency."—Walter How, seaman and sail maker, *Endurance*

1

THE PATH TO LEADERSHIP

He was essentially a fighter, afraid of nothing and of nobody, but, withal, he was human, overflowing with kindness and generosity, affectionate and loyal to all his friends.

—Louis C. Bernacchi, physicist, *Discovery*

THE FIRST CREW

Shackleton grew up among eight sisters and one brother in a family of mixed Quaker and Irish heritage. His upbringing helped shape his leadership style, which was progressive, solicitous, and effective.

From left, in a photo circa 1880, are Kathleen, Ethel, Clara, Amy, Eleanor, Alice, Gladys, and Helen. Ernest is at the top and Frank is seated in front.

W HEN ERNEST SHACKLETON WAS AT THE ZENITH OF HIS
popularity as an explorer, he was invited back to his boys'
school, Dulwich College in London, to present some academic
honors. That was about as close as he ever got to a Dulwich prize,
he joked, to the cheers of the students.

Indeed, Shackleton's early years revealed little promise of the
glories to come. An early biographer, Hugh Robert Mill, a friend
and mentor of the explorer, joked that the only sign in Shackleton's
childhood that he would go to the Antarctic was a class ranking
that was decidedly "south of the equator and sometimes perilously
near the Pole." At the time of the Dulwich speech, a teacher inter-
viewed by a schoolboy magazine remembered the young Shackleton as "a rolling stone." Students and teachers alike saw the boy as
an introvert who was more interested in books than in games yet
who had a hard time with his studies. "He could do better," was a
common refrain in school reports.

One classmate did see a hint of Shackleton in the making. He recalled some forty years after the incident how the young student
had beaten up a schoolyard bully who had been picking on a

smaller boy. From an early age, Shackleton gravitated to the role of protector, stepping up to the front to insist on fair play.

Ernest Henry Shackleton was a natural as a big brother. He was born on February 15, 1874, in Kilkea, County Kildare, Ireland, the second of ten children. He was a healthy and good-looking boy, with slate blue eyes and dark hair. His family and closest friends saw him as humorous, imaginative, and mischievous. By all accounts, he grew up in a loving home surrounded by attentive females. In addition to his eight sisters, his grandmother and aunts often helped his mother with the children. It is no wonder that many people would later remark on his strong feminine sensibilities. Despite a burly physique, enormous stamina, and a tough, no-nonsense manner, he could be nurturing and gentle, quick to forgive frailties, and generous without seeking thanks in return. One friend called him "a Viking with a mother's heart." Both men and women saw this duality in Shackleton and found it irresistible. Shackleton himself was aware of it: "I am a curious mixture with something feminine in me as well as being a man. . . . I have committed all sorts of crimes in thought if not always in action and don't worry much about it, yet I hate to see a child suffer, or to be false in any way."

Shackleton learned from his family
a broad and sympathetic view of the
world that helped shape his leadership style.

The family home had its own split personality, according to Dr. Alexander Macklin, the physician on two of Shackleton's three independent expeditions. He wrote that Shackleton's mother, Henrietta Gavan, was a "warm-hearted and altogether happy-go-lucky" Irishwoman. She was unconventional, keeping her own subscription to the schoolboy publication *Boys Own Paper*. His father, Henry, on the other hand, was "a grave, cautious, solid Yorkshire Quaker." A Shackleton ancestor had migrated to Ireland in the eighteenth century to open a progressive school. The Shackleton family has in it a wide strain of principled individualism that survives to this day.

Shackleton's father settled his family in the lush farmland of County Kildare. When Ernest was six years old, the elder Shackleton moved the family to Dublin, where he studied medicine at Trinity College. He became a physician, a vocation that provided a home with solid, upper-middle-class comforts.

Henry Shackleton headed a strict, though apparently not oppressive, household. The Bible was read aloud in the home, and young Ernest, who had a flair for the dramatic, led his siblings into the children's temperance movement. They would gather outside pubs, singing songs about the perils of alcohol. By then that branch of the family had converted to Church of England, but such youthful activism suggests some vestiges of Quaker culture remained. In the second half of the nineteenth century, Quakers were active worldwide in many progressive political movements: abolition, prison reform, education reform, pacifism, women's suffrage, and the temperance movement, which held that alcohol was a chief cause of family violence and poverty.

Throughout his life, Shackleton was described as being ahead of his time in his attitude toward and treatment of his men. He also encouraged his sisters always to express themselves and to develop their own careers, and they became impressively self-sufficient women for their day, choosing vocations such as artist, midwife, customs officer, and writer. As an adult, Shackleton abandoned temperance and other religious practices and embraced his share of vices. But he maintained his faith and his moral compass, balancing his contemplative, spiritual side with a practical, humanistic commitment. Later in life, Shackleton's wife wrote a bio-graphical note for Dulwich alumni in which she stated her husband was "interested in social welfare movements." Ultimately, his authority as a leader rested on his genuine regard and respect for the men he led.

If Ernest Shackleton had anything in common with his father it was that they both pursued their interests with great passion. The elder Shackleton relished domesticity, never more content than when poring over scientific texts at his last family home in Sydenham in London. He lived there for thirty-two years, tending to his medical practice, his family, and a meticulously kept rose garden. Ernest, by contrast, loved poetry and the sea. He was to become famously incapable of staying put, going to the ends of the earth to seek adventure. What he definitely didn't want was to follow his father's wish that he become a doctor.

Ernest was ten years old when his family moved to England. His spoken English forever retained traces of his Irish roots and so he was always identified, for better or for worse, as an outsider. His Anglo-Irish culture helped shape his independent mindset, giving him a healthy disregard for custom, clan, and class.

In England, Shackleton was sent to school for the first time. He was eleven years old. Until then, his father had educated him and his siblings at home. From the start, Shackleton showed a certain discomfort in a formal classroom setting, and wasn't destined to stay long in it. His first school was Fir Lodge in Croydon, south of London. Shackleton's classmates teased the newcomer, goading him and another Irish boy to fight each other on St. Patrick's Day. The boys gave him the nickname "Micky," and he adopted it for life, signing his name as such in letters to his wife and close friends.

When he was thirteen years old, Shackleton was sent to Dulwich College, a solid boys' school attended mostly by day students who were the children of professionals. He was seen as immature and inattentive to schoolwork, so was often placed with students a year younger. One teacher reported that the young Shackleton "wants waking up." Another predicted, "He has not yet fully exerted himself." A schoolmaster who met Shackleton after he had become a famous explorer confessed, "We never discovered you when you were at Dulwich."

"No," Shackleton replied sympathetically, "but I had not then discovered myself."

Shackleton complained the school didn't make things interesting. Geography was "names of towns, lists of capes and bays and islands," he said. Worse, it took great poets and writers and made them dull by "the dissection, the parsing" of their work. Shackleton seemed a typically moody teen, but he was never disruptive or rebellious. Instead, he plotted an escape. He announced at fifteen years of age that he was going to leave home for life on the seas. "I wanted to be free," he wrote later. "I wanted to escape from a routine which didn't at all agree with my nature and which, therefore, was doing no good to my character. Some boys take to school like ducks to water; for some boys, whether they take to it or not, the discipline is good; but for a few rough spirits the system is chafing, not good, and the sooner they are pitched into the world, the better. I was one of those."

The decision greatly pained Henry Shackleton but he didn't stand in his son's way. Rather, he used family connections to help him secure a decent cabin-boy position. Shackleton's mother encouraged him to pursue his dreams so he would have no regrets later.

Shackleton joined the merchant marine, eventually learning the rugged, freewheeling, commercial culture of the service. He gave notice to the school but finished the 1890 spring term while waiting for his position to be settled. Once he had fixed on a goal and purpose, he at last was motivated to apply himself. He began to excel as a student, shooting up to fifth place in a class of thirty-one boys. It was the awakening his teacher had said he needed. After finishing the term, he traveled to Liverpool and joined the crew of the sailing ship *Hoghton Tower*.

Once his choice was made, Shackleton
saw his commitments through to the end.

Shackleton was homesick and unhappy for most of the four years of his apprenticeship at sea. He had left the protective bosom of his religious, largely female household and had thrown himself into the hard-boiled sailor's world. Initially, he was under no contractual obligation to stay, but he refused to quit. He was determined to complete the difficult apprenticeship and launch a career. "I don't think I ever formulated any definite idea as to what all this rough work was leading up to," he said, "but I dreamed prodigiously about big things ahead, big things in the nature of adventure."

The work was rougher than anything Shackleton had daydreamed about at his desk at school. He swabbed decks, polished brass, and did backbreaking work loading and unloading cargo. Biographer H. R. Mill described one assignment to pick up a shipment of rice from India and bring it to Mauritius: "a horrible job, for every one of the 2,600 bags, each weighing 170 pounds, that were to be loaded each day, had to be passed along the deck from hand to hand." The rough sacks tore at Shackleton's hands and so bruised them that the boy apologized in letters home about his writing having to be so brief and in such poor penmanship. "That such a system of loading cargo could exist even on sailing ships in the last decade of the Victorian age, so renowned for its mechanical achievements, is not a little surprising," Mill wrote.

It was dangerous work. The crew sometimes encountered weeks of violent storms that shredded the ship's sails, carried off lifeboats, and tossed the men about. During the worst storms, the young boys would be lashed to the ship to prevent them from being washed overboard. Shackleton saw a crewman get swept away in one of a relentless series of storms. Nine men were bedridden by accidents then, and Shackleton was nearly crushed by falling tackle. He developed lumbago after spending weeks in wet clothes and a wet bed. He suffered dysentery. Once, when the boys were tied up during rough seas, one of the ship's brutes purposely smashed Shackleton's foot with his heavy boot. Shackleton fell to the deck and sank his teeth into the man's leg—and didn't let go. After that, he was left alone.

Shackleton found much about the crew intolerable. Even allowing for the usual embellishments of a boy's letters home, he complained bitterly to his parents about how much he abhorred the drinking, swearing, and gambling that surrounded him. (He admitted to having picked up smoking.) The ports offered no respite. They were seedy, violent places to the boy, and Shackleton chose to spend his evenings aboard ship under the stars, finding solace in the beauty of nature. He wrote in one letter: "Many a painter would have given half of what he possessed to have been able to catch the fading tints of the red and golden sunset we had last night. . . . All I say is, if you wish to see Nature robed in her mantle of might, look at a storm at sea; if you want to see her robed in her mantle of glory, look at a sunset at sea."

On his first assignment, Shackleton worked under a compassionate captain who invited the apprentices to his dinner table and held Sunday sessions of hymn singing in his cabin. The atmosphere was such that Shackleton, to his amazement, could read his Bible without harassment from his shipmates. Some even joined him.

His next captain, however, was far less kind and ran a ship that was less disciplined and demanded harder work. Shackleton's Bible study made him the object of ridicule by the others. Consequently, he began practicing his religion more privately and let his actions speak for his beliefs.

By his third and last apprentice voyage, he was horribly homesick. To allay his misery on the two-year trip, Shackleton wrote hundreds of letters home and demanded hundreds in return—postcards didn't count.

After completing four years of apprenticeship on clipper ships carrying freight, Shackleton began taking exams every two years to advance to higher posts. By the age of twenty, he had secured a job as third officer on an elite passenger liner. By the age of twenty-four, he had earned his master's certificate, qualifying him to serve as captain of any ship in the merchant marine. He had a new reason to chase success: He was in love with Emily Dorman, a cultured Londoner several years his senior. He wanted a respectable career and the financial security to marry her.

As he matured, Shackleton became more confident and more demanding. He wanted better working conditions, more promising work, and colleagues he could respect. He got what he wanted, thanks to a winning combination of hard work, savvy political instincts, and charm. Early in 1899, he joined the prestigious Union Castle Line. Shackleton figured his new employer would put him in the company of more ambitious peers and well-connected passengers. He worked relentlessly to make contacts and asked for introductions to others. He wasted no time finding a mentor. While serving as fourth officer aboard the *Tantallon Castle,* Shackleton met—and dazzled—a rich steelmaker by the name of Gerald Lysaght. Lysaght was struck by the twenty-five-year-old officer's "unusual character—power and determination" and was convinced that he was destined for great things. For the rest of his life, Shackleton benefited from this patron's financial support of his expeditions.

The force of Shackleton's personality also had a magnetic effect on his superiors and colleagues. The following year, Shackleton was offered the position of fourth mate on the *Tintagel Castle,* a large steamer carrying troops to fight in the Boer War between Great Britain and Dutch colonists in South Africa, but convinced the captain to give him the post of third mate instead. Shackleton distinguished himself in service, going far beyond the basic duties required. He had developed his own ideas of how business should be conducted on a ship and how he would conduct himself. He also started to get a sense of his professional goals.

Shackleton decided to write a book about his experiences, coauthored with the ship's surgeon, Dr. W. McLean. Its unwieldly title tells something of their task: *O.H.M.S.: A Record of the Voyage of the* Tintagel Castle: *Conveying 1,200 Volunteers from Southampton to Cape Town, March 1900.* When he boldly asked the immensely successful writer Rudyard Kipling to write an introductory poem for the book, Kipling obliged. "I will do my level best for you," Shackleton quotes the author as telling him when they met. Shackleton, never one to leave anything to chance, sold the book to readers before it had been written. He took two thousand advance orders, assuring himself a tidy profit. When the book was published in late 1900, the confident Shackleton had a copy specially bound for the queen.

Even after Shackleton became an explorer famous for his incredible stamina, he would speak with pride of how he made it through his difficult initiation to life on the sea and seemed always to carry some sympathy for the suffering apprentice he had been. Years of unhappy apprenticeship had hardened him and at the same time made him more compassionate toward those who became ill, miserable, or homesick. He learned other lessons he never forgot: that a good boss could make the burden of work seem lighter, that refusing to use the best tools available unfairly burdens workers, and that one person could change an entire work environment. Shackleton also learned some things about himself: that he had a love for nature that sometimes was stronger than his love of civilization, that he liked being center stage, and that he craved a big success.

In every job he held, Shackleton helped boost the morale of the crew.

By the time Shackleton joined the *Tintagel Castle*, his more boisterous side had emerged. He had become acutely mindful of the importance of shipboard morale. He couldn't work effectively in a hostile or vulgar atmosphere and doubted that others could either. But he didn't try to convert the unruly crewmen, as he had attempted in his youth. By the age of twenty-six, he had found a better way to get crews to act civilly.

On the *Tintagel Castle*, Shackleton volunteered to teach the military officers signaling. The ship was an unpleasant place to work; it was extremely crowded with troops and staff, and the ship's officers kept a tight rein on discipline. The crew was demoralized. Shackleton took it upon himself to plan diversions for his mates:

sports, concerts, and an elaborate staging of the coming of Father Neptune—a tradition when crossing the equator. Shackleton's efforts lifted the men's spirits and he became, in the words of one crewman, "the life and soul" of the ship. It was the first time anyone had said that about Shackleton, but it would not be the last. He would be known on every ship he served for his penchant for giving nicknames, for organizing activities, for shenanigans, and for quasi-serious experiments.

Over the years, Shackleton also developed an ability to connect with people into a real talent for giving entertaining speeches in a variety of forums—an office, a fundraising dinner, a press interview. But he probably was given credit for being more of a natural hail-fellow-well-met than he really was. Every indication was that he worked hard at creating a public persona. He saw how vital it was to his success to be someone people liked and wanted to be around—and wanted to give money. But Shackleton kept a side to him that yearned to be alone with his books and to enjoy the calm and quiet of wide-open spaces.

Shackleton read broadly
to find wisdom and guidance for all life's journeys.

Shackleton was determined that his abbreviated formal education not handicap him in the world of wealth and power to which he aspired. He taught himself navigation and seamanship, and whatever else he needed to pass the exams for promotion. More important, he read a wide array of literature. A friend described Shackleton's cabin on the *Tintagel Castle*: "On one side a writing table, with the wall behind covered with photos of friends, and on the other wall a bookcase with the signs of a well-read owner, for in it I saw Shakespeare, Longfellow, Darwin, and Dickens, as well as books on navigation." Shackleton crisscrossed the globe in his service to the merchant marine, visiting Europe, South America, the Far East, the Middle East, China, Africa, and the United States.

But nothing opened his mind to the vastness, richness, and complexity of the world the way his books did. They took him beyond the scope of his personal experience.

Shackleton was a lifelong student of history and poetry. In an interview, he suggested how he came to be such an enthusiastic reader after his lackluster performance in school: "I was never much taken with records of battles and sieges, and dynasties, and dethronements, but of the history of a people struggling to be free, of adventurous nations who sent their mariners into unknown seas, and the history of colonization and exploration."

His education intensified when he met Emily Dorman. She introduced him to museums, art, and lectures and sparked in him a deep appreciation for the poetry of Robert Browning, who would be a particular guiding light for Shackleton for the rest of his life. Shackleton's father already had imbued in him a fondness for Alfred Lord Tennyson, England's poet laureate who was so popular at the end of the Victorian age. Browning and Tennyson represented for Shackleton the two main compass points of his world: Tennyson's view was tender and passive; Browning's was bold and hungry for living. "I tell you what I find in Browning is a consistent, a spontaneous optimism," biographer Harold Begbie quoted Shackleton as saying. "No poet ever met the riddle of the universe with a more radiant answer. He knows what the universe expects of man—courage, endurance, faith—faith in the goodness of existence."

Shackleton's reading on many topics made it easy for him to connect to many people through their interests. Years later, when stranded on the ice, he would prod his men into debates about things like the different types of love, the differences between the Orthodox and Catholic churches, the treatment of blacks in America. "I envied him no end in the way he was always apt in any quotation he made, filling an occasion or anything that happened," one of his men, Lionel Greenstreet, said about him.

Shackleton kept an eye on
new horizons, ready to seize opportunities.

Shackleton read with the rest of the world the fascinating news that the *Belgica* had left Punta Arenas, Chile, in December 1897, with plans to become the first scientific expedition to the Antarctic and to take the first photographs of the region. This event set his life on an entirely new course. He saw the potential and anticipated the popularity of Antarctic exploration and set out to acquire a new set of skills. In 1899, he joined the Royal Geographical Society (RGS), where he was exposed to the culture of exploration.

When the RGS and the Royal Society, an independent scientific academy, decided in 1900 that Britain should fund a national Antarctic expedition of its own, Shackleton was ready. He immediately began a hard campaign to go. A new century was dawning, and ambitious men like him saw endless possibilities and changes afoot. Electricity was revolutionizing home life and industry. Steamers had all but replaced sailing ships. With polar exploration, every corner of the world would be known for the first time. And speculation that Antarctica's ice covered valuable resources made the expeditions seem a shortcut to wealth.

The advances made by explorers and scientists stirred the same kind of heady excitement felt at the dawn of the twenty-first century with the expansion of technology and the move into cyberspace: A new, unknown world was up for grabs, and with it a sense that money and fame were easily attainable—and that everyone had a shot at them. The world seemed to be moving faster and faster.

One of Shackleton's crewmen, Thomas Orde-Lees, imagined in 1915 what the world would look like a century later: "No doubt the explorers of 2015, if there is anything left to explore, will not only carry their pocket wireless telephones fitted with wireless telescopes but will also receive their nourishment and warmth by wireless means and also their power to drive their motor sledges, but, of course, there will be an aerial daily excursion to both Poles then."

Shackleton was ready to leave his old career behind. His last commercial voyage was aboard his largest ship yet, the *Caris-brooke Castle*, a passenger ship bound for the Cape of Good Hope. When he returned from the two-month trip in early 1901, he received word that he had been appointed junior officer on the *Discovery*, the Antarctic expedition ship to be led by Robert F. Scott. The news delighted Shackleton. He immediately was thrust into the limelight, where he demonstrated his talents for dealing with the public and courting the press.

The *Discovery* set sail for Antarctica on July 31, 1901, with thirty-eight men, arriving at McMurdo Sound early the following year. The crew's excitement made for a lively voyage. Shackleton had an advantage over most of the other young officers in that he was an experienced sailor. Exploration ships used a combination of sails and steam because the long journey south posed refueling problems. Most of his shipmates had trained on steamers and had to learn sailing techniques.

Shackleton had to learn how to perform scientific experiments. H. R. Mill, the multitalented scientist at the Royal Geographical Society, sailed as far as Madeira to tutor the crew in science. He taught Shackleton how to measure saline levels and water density and perform other tests. He found Shackleton impatient with the precision demanded by scientific work, but otherwise a good student who took criticism well.

Shackleton again was called "the life and soul" of the ship by the *Discovery* crew. He stirred up the crewmen, amusing them with inventions like a sledge with wheels made from rum barrels. All the while he did exceptional work. He was the first member of the expedition to find vegetation; he was the first to spot new land, which was called Edward VII Land; he did a fine job editing the *South Polar Times*, the ship's publication. He also improved the packing of the sledges, having studied the inefficiencies of the crew's first sledging efforts. Suffice it to say that two of his colleagues on that ship, Louis Bernacchi and H. R. Mill, were so taken with the twenty-seven-year-old novice explorer that both wrote about his extraordinary leadership abilities after his death. Mill, who became a close, lifelong friend of Shackleton's, wrote a rich biography.

Scott chose Shackleton and the expedition physician Edward A. Wilson to accompany him on the "Great Southern Journey," an attempt to make the sixteen-hundred-mile trek to the Pole and back that began in November 1902. The long march in the Antarctic cold over treacherous terrain demanded extra heat-giving and strength-building nourishment. Scott, however, skimped on the rations to lighten the loads on the sledges. By Christmas, all three men showed signs of scurvy. They were forced to turn back 460 miles short of the Pole on the last day of the year. Shackleton, in particular, was in a fight for his life. In addition to starvation and scurvy, he was suffering from what appeared to be heart and lung ailments. The bedraggled trio just made it back to the ship on February 3, 1903. Far from feeling sympathetic or even responsible for his stricken colleague, Scott seemed to blame the march's failure on Shackleton's illness.

The *Discovery* expedition may have advanced Antarctic exploration as a whole, but there was little concrete to show for the two-year effort. Worst of all, one seaman died early on in an accident. Overall, Scott was unwilling or unable to adapt his formal naval training to the harsh and unfamiliar environment. Frozen in the waters off the Antarctic, for example, he conducted formal inspection on deck every Sunday. He also made the crew swab the deck, even though the water froze as soon as it hit the boards.

Despite the fact that Shackleton had made a good many of the contributions logged by the *Discovery* crew, in March 1903—halfway through the expedition—Scott demanded that Shackleton volunteer to return home on the relief ship. Shackleton resisted, having by that time been well on the road to recovery. Scott, however, threatened to send him back in disgrace if he didn't declare himself sick.

Shackleton turned a setback into
an opportunity to make a big move on his own.

Shackleton was bitterly disappointed about being sent home. The bad feelings between Scott and Shackleton that developed over the course of the expedition were never mended. But Shackleton never publicly retaliated. Instead, he did his rival one better: He used his early return to steal some thunder from the *Discovery*'s later arrival home. He beguiled the public with dramatic tales of derring-do on the mysterious continent. Shackleton found people had an insatiable curiosity about the South, and he took full advantage of it. The publicity helped burnish his reputation as an expert expedition planner. He was called upon to help the Argentine government plan an Antarctic relief expedition to leave supplies on Paulet Island. At about the same time, he helped organize the transport of ten thousand Russian soldiers to the front during the Russo-Japanese war.

Shackleton also tried a series of other jobs, though all with the intent of using what he learned and earned to further his career in exploration. He first tried his hand at journalism, editing copy at *Royal Magazine*, where his boss was clearly smitten with his charm. The editor said Shackleton's enthusiasm and creative thinking would have been valuable in any workplace. "I am convinced that if he had gone to a stock-broker, a butcher, a carpenter, or a theatrical manager and asked for a job, he would have got it. There was something about him that compelled confidence," F. W. Everett explained. "And none of these good folk would have regretted taking him on. Though stock-broking and acting may have been as little in his line as journalism, he would have made his mark in them somehow or other. . . . He was brimming over with original, unconventional, racy ideas, which, whether practical or not, were always stimulating and suggestive."

Shackleton used his three months at the magazine to make valuable connections and to learn how to handle the press. He had donated fees from one article to the *Discovery* Relief Fund. Scott's ship had become trapped in the Antarctic ice, and had to be dynamited out in February 1904 at great expense.

Using his contacts at the RGS, Shackleton then moved to Edinburgh and became an influential officer of the Royal Scottish Geographical Society. He made his mark there too. As the new secretary of the society, he was credited with boosting membership by five hundred.

By this time, his finances had improved sufficently to marry Emily Dorman—on April 9, 1904. The couple would go on to have three children: Raymond, Cecily, and Edward. Emily never got used to the long separations and disruptions of their family life. Shackleton's letters to her over the years are full of repeated promises to give up exploration, and repeated apologies for not doing so. Still, the couple remained together, and Emily never remarried after her husband's death.

Shackleton even dabbled—unsuccessfully—in politics. He felt he was popular enough to try a run for Parliament as a Liberal-Unionist for Dundee in the 1906 elections. He was a crowd pleaser but didn't pull in votes. He was soundly defeated. After the election, he became an assistant to William Beardmore, a Glasgow engineering magnate who introduced Shackleton to a circle of prominent businessmen.

All these pursuits were but a prelude to Shackleton's inevitable return to the Antarctic. For him nothing matched the thrill or satisfaction of exploration. The pull was irresistible. Polar explorers were the celebrities of their day—their exploits chronicled in the new medium of motion pictures. Shackleton hatched plans to lead his own Antarctic expedition in 1907. Beardmore helped outfit the ship, named the *Nimrod*. Fame and fortune seemed at hand, although fame came much easier than fortune. Shackleton's plans for an independent voyage created enough of a stir that King Edward VII and Queen Alexandra took a personal interest in the charming and modern young explorer and visited him on the Nimrod to wish him well. The queen, particularly taken with Shackleton, gave him a Union Jack to plant at the South Pole.

The outfitting of men and ships for the difficult journey was costly, and despite the royal attention, funds for polar research were hard to come by. The British establishment wanted the Royal Navy to make its mark in exploration and didn't welcome intrusion by independents. What little public funding was available was very competitive. Shackleton had to work hard to get industrialists to part with their money.

For all his frustration, Shackleton never oversold the *Nimrod* expedition to his backers. He made his plans and his goals clear. The ship would sail from New Zealand and drop off a shore party in the Antarctic in February 1908. It would head back to New Zealand and return in early 1909 to retrieve the men. One party would travel east to explore King Edward VII Land; one would go west to find the Magnetic South Pole; and the main party would search for the geographic South Pole. The expedition would try various innovations in hauling, such as using hardy Manchurian ponies instead of dogs, and would test a specially designed motorcar. Provisions for the southern journey were to be laid down every one hundred miles for use on the return trip.

In a letter to Emily, written en route to the Antarctic in 1907, Shackleton said that she should be proud of his chance to do great work. "There are thousands who would give their eyes to go; and this expedition owes nothing to the world at large and yet it may help the honor of the country," he wrote. He said he hoped the trip would relieve him of the necessity of "having to grind away" in business year after year while saving only a little money. If successful, he said, "there will be plenty for us to live our lives as we wish."

Shackleton was bold in his plans,
but cautious in their execution, paying close attention to details.

Shackleton was aware of the ill-conceived plans that had plagued
prior polar exploration, disheartening even the most enthusiastic
explorers. Accordingly, he sought a reputation not for bravado—
anyone tackling the Antarctic was credited with having a lot of
guts—but for caution. He often referred to himself as "Old Cautious," and was delighted when others did too. It was not neces-
sarily the first adjective that came to mind when people thought of
Shackleton, but men in his command all knew he was careful in his
work and concerned about the safety of all. This reputation was
particularly important when raising funds from private sources,
which wanted some assurance that their investment wouldn't
wind up on the bottom of the sea.

On the *Nimrod*, Shackleton would be the one to take care of an
ailing crew member or break in a team of dogs. H. R. Mill saw
Shackleton's meticulous attention to details as further evidence of
the duality in his nature: "A mind given to exhaustive foresight and
the mechanical provision of routine wants is rarely attracted to
dangerous enterprises, hence the usual arrangement of a learned
society or a cautious committee to plan and equip an expedition,
and a daring fellow to carry it out under the restraint of prudent instructions. The best explorer, however, is the man who can both
'conceive and dare,' who carries his organizing committee with him
on his own feet, and knows that there is [no one] to blame for failure but himself. To such an explorer is due on his return the undi-
vided praise for plan and execution." That explorer was Shackleton.

Shackleton learned from past mistakes.
Experience taught him the kind of leader he didn't want to be.

Like all great pathfinders, Shackleton studied the past while he
dreamed of the future. He extracted what was valuable in earlier ex-

peditions that he could use, identified problems that he could solve, and pushed himself to innovate.

The *Nimrod* crew called Shackleton "the Boss," and it stuck with him the rest of his life. He learned how to select a crew, to conceive and execute scientific experiments and observations, and to adapt plans to fit changing needs. His longstanding convictions—the belief in putting the welfare of his men first and respecting each individual—remained admirably steadfast, even as his popularity grew and the burdens on his performance increased. "He is a marvelous man, and I would follow him anywhere," wrote the *Nimrod*'s engineer, Harry Dunlop, in a letter to a friend.

Shackleton set out on the *Nimrod* expedition to make a name for himself and to distinguish himself from his rival, Scott. He was careful to show respect for Scott's contributions, but was determined to set higher standards. He bragged in a letter to Emily that the *Nimrod* ship was better, though smaller, than the *Discovery* and boasted that he had supplied it expertly and assembled a carefully chosen crew.

In Scott, Shackleton had a portrait of exactly the kind of leader he didn't want to be. Scott, trained in the British Royal Navy, was rigid and formal. For him, the prize was always paramount, and his military training would have dictated that some loss of life was inevitable. He preferred to hire men of like discipline for his expeditions, sometimes with unfortunate results. "Orders are orders in the Navy and we had been ordered to remain where we were," Frank Wild wrote about one experience he had as a member of the *Discovery* crew. "Although we were all chilled to the bone and one man badly frostbitten and staying there would have inevitably been the death of us all in a few hours, it was a long time before I could persuade the others to move on and try to find the ship."

Scott was dour, bullying, and controlling; Shackleton was warm, humorous, and egalitarian. Scott was known to torment his underlings; Shackleton would tease but never humiliate. Scott tried to orchestrate every movement of his men; Shackleton gave his men responsibility and some measure of independence. Scott was secretive and untrusting; Shackleton talked openly and frankly with the men about all aspects of the work. Scott put his team at risk to achieve his goals; Shackleton valued his men's lives above all else.

On the *Nimrod* expedition, when the men had set up a winter camp on the Antarctic coast, Shackleton made the hut into a home. It was crowded, cluttered, and hard to keep clean, but the men never became disgruntled or depressed. Raymond Priestley wrote, "In the long winter months, when the scientists toiled in darkness and cold at their routine tasks outside, the help and company of our leader might always be relied upon."

Shackleton was a sociable man but that didn't mean he allowed lax discipline. For example, while trying to find a suitable Antarctic landing site, the captain of the *Nimrod*, Rupert England, drove everyone to distraction with his nervous maneuvering of the ship. Yet when someone publicly made a derogatory remark about the captain, Shackleton became furious, reminding the crew that they must respect the captain's authority as dictated by the rules of the sea. He did so even though he also had concluded that the captain was compromising the safety of the men, and had written to his agent in New Zealand asking him to select a replacement to retrieve the crew in the spring.

Shackleton was new in his leadership post, however, and made several mistakes. He sometimes had a hard time facing his men, procrastinating, for example, before telling the injured Philip Brocklehurst he couldn't go on the march to the Pole. Brocklehurst's mother had bought the nineteen-year-old a place on the expedition and Shackleton felt beholden to him. He also could be indecisive. Dr. Marshall had his own take on Shackleton's feminine side, calling him a "little old lady" for being overly cautious. Even if the criticism was uncalled for, it showed Shackleton's inexperience at handling dissenters.

Shackleton, however, was a quick study and knew he had to find another way to lead his educated crew, who did not respond well to strict discipline and demanded to be heard. Shackleton also noted at least three mistakes that he would have to correct on his next expedition: The ponies were too heavy for the icy terrain; the food needed to be even more nutritious and more compact for the journeys inland; and key crew members didn't share his temperament and vision.

Shackleton always put
the well-being of his crew first.

Shackleton always weighed the cost of a goal against the expense of reaching it. He didn't believe in Pyrrhic victories. He preferred to replace a failed goal with an attempt at another, more ambitious one.

Shackleton and his three companions—Dr. Eric Marshall, Lt. Jameson Boyd Adams, and Frank Wild—set out for the Pole on November 3, 1908, carrying enough food for ninety-one days. By November 26 they already had beaten the record achieved by the *Discovery* team, although Wild's diary shows he was beginning to doubt whether they could make it to the Pole and back before their relief ship left at the end of February. Wild almost didn't make it at all. He was nearly killed when the last of the team's four ponies fell into a crevasse, pulling him with it. That misfortune virtually ruled out the possibility of reaching the Pole. Without the pony's meat, the men were desperately short of food. They trudged on for another month, Shackleton noting in his diary that "difficulties are just things to overcome after all."

On January 9, 1909, they made a final dash to the South, planting the flag donated by Queen Alexandra at 88 degrees 23 minutes south—just ninety-seven miles from the South Pole. They could go no farther. Wild said Shackleton had "strained every muscle and nerve to the limit" to get that far, as he would see him push himself to his limits time and again in the twenty years he knew him. The Boss gave up his quest to ensure the whole party returned alive.

The men had to race back to the ship before they starved. They ate the last bit of pony meat from their stores. It turned out to be spoiled and the four became violently ill with dysentery. At one point, they were too weak to even strike a camp. Fearing death was at hand, Shackleton asked Wild to sing his favorite hymn, "Lead Kindly Light." Wild couldn't manage more than the first verse:

> Lead, kindly Light! amid the encircling gloom,
> Lead thou me on;
> The night is dark, and I am far from home,
> Lead thou me on:
> Keep thou my feet; I do not ask to see
> The distant scene; one step enough for me.

Slowly, the men began to recover from the illness, but they were running out of time to make it back to the ship. Shackleton pushed Wild to take his breakfast biscuit, insisting that his friend needed it more than he did. When Wild refused, the Boss threatened to bury it in the snow rather than eat it himself. Wild took the biscuit. It was a gesture he never forgot.

Just short of starvation, the four men reached a richly stocked depot that a supporting party from the *Nimrod* had laid for them. Dr. Marshall stuffed himself until he became sick. A blizzard pinned them inside the tent for a day, but the doctor still was not well enough to make the thirty-three-mile dash back to the ship. The Boss had left instructions for the *Nimrod*'s new captain to sail if the team hadn't returned by February 28. He and Wild would have to race ahead to meet the deadline. Leaving Marshall and Adams behind, Shackleton and Wild set out. A mile from the camp, Shackleton took Wild's hand. "Frank, old man," he said, "it's the old dog for the hard road every time." Wild, in his unpublished memoirs, pointed out with pleasure that the two "old dogs" were thirty-five years old and the two left behind were in their twenties.

Shackleton and Wild struggled to within three miles of their base, then realized they were on the other side of the inlet and it wasn't frozen solid as they had hoped. They dropped their tent, cooking gear, and sleeping bags, and pushed themselves to make a laborious crossing of a one-thousand-foot glacier, arriving at the hut on the very last day Shackleton had calculated for their return. They were dismayed to find a letter nailed to the hut, explaining that the Magnetic Pole party had accomplished its goal and that the ship had left two days ahead of schedule to seek better shelter. That meant it would be almost a year before another ship could return for the rescue.

With the strength of mind, optimism, and determination that characterized his best moments, Shackleton refused to give in to despair despite all the evidence pointing to doom. He and Wild set about trying to signal the ship. Their fingers were too frozen to tie a knot to hoist a flag, but eventually they managed to start a fire using timbers from the hut. Without sleeping bags they were too cold to sleep, so they went into the hut's photography darkroom and lit a portable Primus stove, nearly asphyxiating themselves with the fumes. By the next morning a rescue was under way. The night before, Aeneas Mackintosh, aboard the *Nimrod*, had been overcome with a feeling that Shackleton had made it to the coast. At midnight, acting on his hunch, he climbed the masthead to have a look back and spotted their fire.

Their rescue came at no thanks to the ship's captain, who had been hired to replace the original one. Though he nearly cost Shackleton and his three companions their lives, the Boss never took him to task, nor mentioned the incident again. Now that two captains had failed him, the Boss would be very careful about selecting his next one.

Shackleton and Wild were rescued on March 1. Although Shackleton had just gone for two nights without sleep and had endured four months of unbelievable physical hardship, he turned around a mere three hours after reaching the ship and insisted on leading the relief party to retrieve Marshall and Adams. What's more, Shackleton took charge of all the cooking on the trip. Two days later, they returned with the two stragglers. Once aboard the *Nimrod* again, all three of the relief party collapsed into bed while Shackleton, who hadn't slept during the rescue, went to the bridge to guide the ship out to the open sea. In the end, the Boss covered ninety-nine miles in four days.

The achievements of the *Nimrod*'s British Antarctic Expedition were impressive. Within five weeks of landing in the Antarctic, expedition members had become the first to climb the volcano Mount Erebus, 13,350 feet high. During the winter in the base camp on Cape Royds in McMurdo Sound, the group wrote and printed a book, the *Aurora Australis*. (Shackleton had sent two men to learn typesetting, printing, and lithography in a crash three-week course.) The one hundred copies that were printed became instant treasures.

Even more significant was that on January 16, 1909, a team of three had reached the Magnetic South Pole. The men had trudged a total of 1,260 miles in 122 days to make the journey and return to base. Most important, however, the Boss's team had gotten closer to the geographic South Pole than anyone else. They had marched 1,740 miles, pulling a sledge most of the way, on short rations and little sleep.

Shackleton had bested Scott's record for Farthest South by 357 miles. He pulled ahead of the pack of his fellow explorers, and his fame extended throughout the world. He was knighted and showered with awards from many countries. He was also very much in demand as a public speaker and became a successful lecturer. He toured in Italy, Austria, Hungary, Germany, Russia, Canada, and the United States. Often, he had his lecture translated into the local language and then read it to great effect, if with a halting accent. He once boasted that he was sure he could deliver his speech in Chinese, as he had picked up a few words of that language during his early travels in the merchant marine. Despite his popularity, his fees didn't begin to cover the expenses of the *Nimrod*. It took him years to pay off the expedition's debts.

Shackleton was hailed as a leader as well as an adventurer for his *Nimrod* achievements. On June 14, 1909, *The Daily Mirror* in London printed a story by a reporter who spent two days with Shackleton on his trip home from the expedition. Under the banner headline "LIEUTENANT SHACKLETON'S HOMECOMING" was a subhead that declared he was "A MAN BORN TO RULE."

Shackleton wrote a book about his *Nimrod* adventure. H. R. Mill described *The Heart of the Antarctic* as "the richest array of illustrations that ever graced a book of travel since the photographic era came in." It was used to teach English classes in Holland.

In America, Shackleton was invited to Taft's White House and was awarded a gold medal by the National Geographic Society before an audience of five thousand. He received another medal from Admiral Robert Peary at the American Geographical Society and was warmly received at Harvard with a lusty college cheer. That year, he also made a recording describing *Nimrod*. It was typical Shackleton: He spoke first of the expedition's achievements, then gave the names of his fourteen comrades so that they might share the credit, and ended with an edited version of "The Lone Trail," a poem by Robert W. Service about taking the road less traveled:

> *The trails of the world be countless, and most of the trails be tried:*
> *You tread on the heels of the many, till you come where the ways*
>   *divide;*
> *And one lies safe in the sunlight, and the other is dreary and wan,*
> *Yet you look aslant at the Lone Trail, yet the Lone Trail lures you on.*

As much as Shackleton enjoyed the spotlight, he hated being called a hero. When the *Nimrod* story was being published as a reading book for schools, Shackleton refused to let it be titled, *The Hero Readers*. Many who knew Shackleton say he actually became more personable and self-effacing after he became famous. "Though still a young man, Shackleton seems to have taken all this heady stuff with surprising modesty," Dr. Macklin wrote later. "He never became the least conceited; indeed he was too big a man ever to have done so."

Shackleton avoided public fights,

engaging always in respectful competition with rivals.

Polar exploration was a matter of national pride. The Japanese, Norwegians, Germans, and Australians were all racing for the Pole and other destinations in the Antarctic and explorers waved the flag to whip up enthusiasm for their expeditions. Shackleton, though, felt a brotherhood with the other explorers and believed the realities of the exploration business meant they would have to cooperate with each other at some point. He looked to them for new ideas and offered them his in return.

In fact, his biggest rival was his countryman Scott, but Shackleton kept his feelings about his old nemesis to himself. When Scott announced he was going to take the *Terra Nova* to the Antarctic in another bid for the Pole, for example, Shackleton told Frank Wild that he would sit on the sidelines for a time and let Scott take a crack at it. Shackleton even helped Scott launch his expedition in 1910, lending a hand in organizing the provisions. He also helped equip expeditions from other countries, sharing what he had learned about packing and calculating what was needed for survival.

In one letter of unclear destination, dated 1903, Shackleton wrote: "I see that you are intending to take an Expedition to the North Pole, so as I am greatly interested in all these undertakings, I would be very glad to give you any assistance in my power to enable you to fit out or get the ideas of equipment for this sort of thing. My experience with the National Antarctic Expedition enables me perhaps to be of use, and so as a member of the Southern Sledge journey and therefore dealing with dogs, some information might be useful, besides which I have just fitted out the *Terra Nova* for the Admiralty. Being conversant with the stores necessary I might help you.

"I should be glad to see you at any time, and please understand that this is only for the regard that one explorer has for another, for there is no money question in it."

Just as Scott was organizing his expedition, Roald Amundsen of Norway was sailing for what he had told his men—and the world— would be a five-year trek across the North Pole. He changed course, however, and at Madeira disclosed that his actual destination was the South Pole. The race was on. Arriving at Antarctica, he charted a new route to the South Pole. He reached it on December 14, 1911.

"Heartiest congratulations. Magnificent achievement" was the cable Shackleton sent to Amundsen. He refused to play down the achievement as the British establishment was doing, writing in the press that he believed the Norwegians would have paid tribute to Scott had he been the first.

Maintaining the good will of fellow explorers paid off when it came time for Shackleton to write a prospectus for his *Endurance* expedition. He got glowing recommendations from the most successful explorers of his day. Amundsen wrote: "If you succeed in your brilliant enterprise (which I am sure you will) you certainly will have done your share of the work and added the most beautiful stone to the magnificent crown won by the hardy and enterprising British explorers."

Admiral Robert Peary added: "The idea is splendid. . . . he is undoubtedly the best man in Great Britain for the task, and his previous work in these regions have given him just the experience necessary to carry the expedition to a successful conclusion."

From 1910 until the summer of 1913, when he began organizing the transcontinental *Endurance* expedition, Shackleton threw himself as best he could into domestic life. He also dabbled in a variety of business ventures, all designed to return a quick profit to fund further explorations. He invested in such risky ventures as selling elegant cigarettes to Americans, building a taxi fleet in Bulgaria, and mining gold in Hungary.

In April 1912 the shocking news came that the *Titanic* had sunk, killing fifteen hundred people. Shackleton was asked to give testimony at the official inquiries as an expert on navigating icy waters. He absolved the shipmaster, saying the biggest problem was that the ship's owners were on board, pushing for a faster and faster voyage.

More shocking news followed: Scott and his four companions had died early that year on their trek back from the Pole, having arrived one month after Amundsen's party. The public became obsessed with Scott's sacrifice, which fit the romantic image of the Victorian-age hero. Maybe others had beaten him to the Pole, the public reasoned, but he had paved the way and paid the ultimate price for it. Shackleton paid tribute to Scott, and given the grim circumstances, it was fortunate that he had never positioned himself as his enemy.

Shackleton was desperate to return to the Antarctic, which was never far from his mind. His business dealings mostly had soured and were nothing but a headache. "All the troubles of the South are nothing to day after day of business," he said.

SHACKLETON'S WAY
OF DEVELOPING LEADERSHIP SKILLS

- Cultivate a sense of compassion and responsibility for others. You have a bigger impact on the lives of those under you than you can imagine.

- Once you make a career decision, commit to stick through the tough learning period.

- Do your part to help create an upbeat environment at work. A positive and cheerful workplace is important to productivity.

- Broaden your cultural and social horizons beyond your usual experiences. Learning to see things from different perspectives will give you greater flexibility in problem solving at work.

- In a rapidly changing world, be willing to venture in new directions to seize new opportunities and learn new skills.

- Find a way to turn setbacks and failures to your advantage. This would be a good time to step forward on your own.

- Be bold in vision and careful in planning. Dare to try something new, but be meticulous enough in your proposal to give your ideas a good chance of succeeding.

- Learn from past mistakes—yours and those made by others. Sometimes the best teachers are the bad bosses and the negative experiences.

- Never insist on reaching a goal at any cost. It must be achieved at a reasonable expense, without undue hardship for your staff.

- Don't be drawn into public disputes with rivals. Rather, engage in respectful competition. You may need their cooperation some day.

WORKING IT IN

Richard Danzig, appointed U.S. secretary of the navy in 1998, was so impressed with Shackleton as a model of good leadership that he held a seminar on the explorer's *Endurance* expedition in December 1999. About seventy invited guests attended, including the deputy secretary of defense, senior naval officers, and senior civilians in the Pentagon.

"The values of leadership he provides are eternal," says Secretary Danzig. "They're derived from the nature of human character and involve making bold ventures and bringing out the best in human beings."

The secretary discovered Shackleton years ago reading Alfred Lansing's *Endurance*. He is convinced that Shackleton's knowledge of a wide variety of literature contributed to the explorer's success as a leader. Mr. Danzig gives copies of the *Endurance* story—among other books—to navy and marine officers, as well as visiting dignitaries. "One of the great advantages of reading fiction or history is it gives you the opportunity to understand the world from different vantage points and different time periods and different psychologies," he says. "That's important to a leader, so one of my prime aims in distributing books is to get people to think outside themselves and to think broadly."

The secretary wrote an article for the *Marine Corps Gazette* in 1999 recommending works of twentieth-century fiction and nonfiction. They were: *Gates of Fire* by Stephen Pressfield about the Spartan battle at Thermopylae in 480 B.C.; *I, Claudius* and *Claudius the God,* books by Robert Graves about the Roman emperor; *Shōgun* by James Clavell about an Englishman in seventeenth-century Japan; *Lord Jim* by Joseph Conrad about a sailor's loss of honor; *All the King's Men* by Robert Penn Warren about a young man's loss of innocence amid the politics of 1930s Louisiana; and *Generations of Winter* by Vassily Aksyonov about a Russian family's survival in a totalitarian state.

The secretary says he uses the *Endurance* story to illustrate the kind of leadership he wants to encourage in the navy and marine corps, which he oversees. For him, the Shackleton model works on many levels: leadership in response to danger and adversity, working in extreme environments, surviving unforeseen challenges, flexibility in planning, and gaining and retaining the loyalty of those in your command. Through great danger and under tremendous pressure, the explorer kept his crew together, maintained morale, and improved on his escape plans until he got everyone to safety, Mr. Danzig says. He particularly admires what he identifies as Shackleton's thoughtfulness, in every sense of the word: "He was thoughtful in the emotional sense—he was empathetic and caring. He was also thoughtful in the cognitive sense—he thought logically even while under great stress."

Mr. Danzig believes Shackleton had some flaws. "He is not the complete leader," he says, "but he is an exceptional example of a set of traits that we highly value. . . . Warfare constantly requires adaptation and innovation, and he was extraordinary in that."

Mr. Danzig, as a top manager of the Pentagon, has made some astute observations about the nature of organizations. In the February/March 2000 issue of the magazine *Civilization*, he was quoted as saying, "Organizations are a kind of fossil record of what bothered their predecessors." That record should be studied, he argues, to better anticipate how organizations will change. "The issue is not whether they will encounter different types of crises; they will. The issue is whether or not they will change fast enough to be prepared for those crises when they occur."

Still, Mr. Danzig, a student of history, warns against what he calls "overlearning" from the past; that is, looking too much at one set of circumstances instead of contemplating all the possibilities and discontinuities one might face in current situations. Likewise, he is not particularly confident of anyone's ability to predict the future. So he is interested in highly flexible strategies. For that reason, he admires the way Shackleton mapped out several alternative step-by-step plans for the rescue of his men. "There was no glossing over of the situation," he says. "Shackleton came to grips with the cold, hard realities and constantly generated options that offered his group ways of getting out."

Secretary Danzig has written broadly on the subjects of law, national security, and leadership, especially leadership during crisis. He received a doctorate of law from Yale and a Ph.D. in history from Oxford University, where he was also a Rhodes scholar. He served as a law clerk to Supreme Court Justice Byron White, and went on to teach law at Stanford and Harvard. In 1979 he left academia to work in deputy assistant posts under the secretary of defense. Later, he became a partner in the Washington-based law firm Latham & Watkins. He left the firm to serve as an undersecretary of the navy from 1993 to 1997. While in that post he helped integrate the functions of the navy and marine corps, reducing the size of his department, developing a program to increase minority participation in the officer ranks, and making available online systems of information. His honors include the Defense Distinguished Service and the Navy Distinguished Service awards.

Mr. Danzig looks to Shackleton for examples of how to build the loyalty of those under one's command. Shackleton's commitment to his men was total, and he protected them from physical and psychological harm. The stranded explorer had to deal with the gamut of human emotions, including fear, anger, and despair, Mr. Danzig observes. "At the same time, the men had only one asset, and that was each other. There were no other people for thousands of miles. In that circumstance, the pressures of that situation, you could either fracture and divide or weld into a tight group. Shackleton's amazing achievement is he always got things to go in the direction of staying together."

Today's military, Secretary Danzig says, emphasizes recruitment, but the greater challenge is retention of good people. He says he is trying to rid the military of the "conscript mentality," the notion that the leadership will always have an unlimited quantity of low-cost labor. His goals are to provide them with better tools, better working conditions, and automation where it can relieve burdens.

In 1999, he helped get Congress to approve the largest pay raise for the navy and marine corps in fifteen years. He also reversed the "zero defect" promotion policy, in order to advance "the best people, not the most immaculate records."

He says his own philosophy of how troops should be treated follows the Shackleton tradition and is another reason he held the seminar on the explorer. He says he has tried to instill among navy and marine officers "a richer sense that our enlisted people are professionals, and that they should be treasured, and their loyalty earned and retained."

2

HIRING AN OUTSTANDING CREW

There was nothing petty in his own nature. The one thing he demanded was cheerfulness from us all; and what he received from every man serving under him was absolute loyalty.

—Leonard D. A. Hussey, meteorologist, *Endurance*

DOWN TO BUSINESS

Even the greatest endeavors begin with the nuts and bolts of doing business. Shackleton was photographed in London on December 30, 1913, the day after announcing his plans for the *Endurance* expedition. This photo appeared on the front page of *The Daily Mirror;* the caption noted that Sir Ernest was the only person not wearing an overcoat in the frigid winter air.

S HACKLETON'S TALENT IN BUSINESS WAS HIS GENIUS FOR raising funds. As an independent explorer he received only modest aid from the British government and geographical societies and had to rely on private sources. In one way, this was an advantage for Shackleton: He was forced to run lean, focused expeditions with a streamlined crew. Shackleton managed to raise as much as $10 million, in today's currency, for each of his independent voyages. He did it by offering London's wealthiest men and women vicarious thrills in exploration and the pride of having their names on various glaciers, promontories, and lifeboats.

The Boss, however, wasn't very good at making money in traditional business. The success of the *Nimrod* had pulled him out of the rat race for the most part, and he came to dislike intensely the daily grind of office work, especially where budgets were concerned. He had talked about giving up his career in exploration, but couldn't bring himself to do it. And why should he? He had found the winning formula: the work he loved most was the thing that he did best and that brought him the most financial reward—plus it made him hugely famous.

In early 1914, Shackleton opened headquarters for the *En-*

durance expedition, officially named the Imperial Trans-Antarctic Expedition, at No. 4 New Burlington Street, in the bustling Piccadilly area of London that had become a favored area for expedition offices. For the voyage, he bought a 144-foot Norwegian-built wooden ship with three masts and a coal-fired steam engine. It had been originally commissioned for a commercial polar-travel venture that was later scratched. Shackleton renamed it *Endurance*. As for other preparations, his main tasks were threefold: The first was to find good men for the journey; the second, to outline a scientific program; the third, to organize equipment. The first task he enjoyed; the others he felt were his duty; all of them he did extremely well.

This time, everyone wanted to work for the great explorer. When Shackleton announced his plans to return to the Antarctic in a letter to *The Times* in London on December 29, 1913, he was deluged with requests. Nearly five thousand hopefuls sent applications, compared with just four hundred for the *Nimrod* seven years earlier. From the thousands, he hired about thirty men to fill the crews for the *Endurance* and the *Aurora*, the expedition's second ship. The second crew, which came to be known as the Ross Sea party, would approach the Antarctic opposite the continent from the *Endurance*'s landing spot and lay food depots for Shackleton's transcontinental team. Shackleton didn't take advantage of the labor glut. He paid his officers slightly above scale.

Amundsen's success and the tragic death of Robert F. Scott and his party had damped British enthusiasm for polar exploration. Shackleton, however, was able to rekindle interest with his idea of achieving the first crossing of the continent on foot, using dogs and sledges, from the Weddell Sea to the Ross Sea. It was an ambitious goal—the last great prize of the age of exploration—and one he ultimately failed to reach. It wasn't until some forty years later that British explorer Vivian Fuchs crossed the continent—with the support of Sir Edmund Hillary—and he used motor vehicles.

Marketers and business-school professors have long told the

story of how the Imperial Trans-Antarctic Expedition got its applicants by running the most successful want ad in history: "Men wanted for Hazardous Journey. Small wages, bitter cold, long months of complete darkness, constant danger. Safe return doubtful. Honour and recognition in case of success." The ad, however, is apocryphal, as no copy has ever been found. Besides, would the optimistic Shackleton ever have doubted a safe return? Rather, the ad was probably the invention of someone amused by the long lines applying for such a horrific assignment.

There was good reason for the enthusiasm. Explorers were the heroes of their day, envied for their chance to bring honor to themselves and their country. Raymond Priestley was one of the many young men who fled the workaday world for the romance of exploration. He had left his studies at Bristol University to join Shackleton on his first independent expedition, as *Nimrod*'s geologist. Later in life, he described what it was like to be one of the chosen: "A well-advertised expedition—especially when, as in my exploring days, the objective was the Pole—was an object of interest and admiration to everyone around. Before they had had a chance to justify themselves, the men were fêted, wined and dined, exposed to flattery and special attention, listened to with respect as authorities on subjects of which they often knew little enough." For their leader, the benefits were magnified many times over.

Life on polar expeditions, however, wasn't for dreamers. Antarctica is the coldest, windiest, and driest continent on earth, covered by a layer of ice up to three miles thick. It snows only one or two inches a year in the frozen desert. Fierce winds consistently whip up the dry snow, which feels more like sand. The lowest temperature ever recorded on earth was in the Antarctic, -128.6 degrees Fahrenheit (-89.2 degrees Celsius), though the mean annual temperature near the South Pole is about -70 degrees Fahrenheit.

Polar expeditions were typically made up of two distinct groups: the shore party of explorers and scientists, and the ship's crew of officers and seamen. On Shackleton's *Nimrod* expedition, for example, the ship dropped off the members of the shore party and their supplies, sailed back to New Zealand for the winter, and returned the following summer to pick up the men. Shackleton's original plan was for the *Endurance* to send the ship to South America for the winter. At South Georgia, however, he changed his mind and decided to keep the ship in the Weddell Sea.

After landing in the Antarctic, a shore party would quickly establish a base camp. The men would make some initial exploratory forays, then spend the winter months fine-tuning their equipment and plans for their projects. As soon as the polar spring arrived the party would divide into smaller groups and set out in different directions to achieve their own goals, working through the summer.

Most of the scientists and professionals who joined polar expeditions were young men who had led comfortable lives. They had every intention of settling back into their homes and careers after one or two adventures. Most were unprepared for the solitude and rigors of the work, which complicated the task of selecting a compatible team. Of utmost importance was determining a man's disposition and character. In *The Heart of the Antarctic*, his account of the *Nimrod* expedition, Shackleton described the task of putting together an ideal crew: "The men selected must be qualified for the work, and they must also have the special qualifications required to meet polar conditions. They must be able to live together in harmony for a long period of time without outside communication, and it must be remembered that the men whose desires lead them to the untrodden paths of the world have generally marked individuality. It was no easy matter for me to select the staff."

Shackleton once recalled what a London theatrical manager had told him about the challenge of forming a repertory company: "Character and temperament matter quite as much as acting ability."

"Just my problem," Shackleton responded. "I have to balance my types, too, and their science or seamanship weighs little against the kind of chaps they were."

The Boss built his crew
around a core of experienced workers.

After *Nimrod*, Shackleton wanted the "old dogs" for the toughest work. He also needed them to help establish a professional atmosphere. The young men were hardy and enthusiastic, but when things got scary they seemed quicker to panic or resign themselves to the situation. It wasn't easy finding experienced men; Antarctic exploration was new and old hands seldom wanted to keep returning to the continent. Shackleton began his search by approaching those he knew from past expeditions, then added candidates recommended by colleagues.

When Shackleton was hiring for the *Nimrod* expedition in 1907, he offered positions to nine veterans of Scott's *Discovery* voyage. For various reasons, including prior commitments and loyalty to Scott, only two accepted. After Shackleton had made a name for himself, each subsequent expedition drew increasing numbers of repeat applicants. Four members of the *Nimrod* expedition joined the Imperial Trans-Antarctic Expedition. Amazingly, eight men from the embattled *Endurance* expedition signed up for what would be Shackleton's last voyage, aboard the *Quest*.

Shackleton raised some eyebrows when he hired fifty-year-old T. W. Edgeworth David, a geology professor at Sydney University, for the *Nimrod*. He was twice the age of many on the crew. The Boss correctly predicted that the scientist's calm would be "a great influence for good amongst the younger men." He also knew he needed someone with exceptional experience to coordinate the various scientific projects that were being done, which the professor did very well and Shackleton didn't have the expertise to handle.

One of the two men who joined the *Endurance* from the *Discovery* was Tom Crean. Crean also went on Scott's *Terra Nova* expedition, after which he was awarded the Albert medal. He had saved the life of Lt. Edward Evans, who was dying of scurvy, by dashing ahead to the ship for help. Crean had previously had an erratic career in the British Royal Navy, where several promotions were interrupted by a demotion for drunkenness and unbecoming behavior. Scott took him on as a seaman. Shackleton, however, saw a great potential in the valorous, if somewhat rough-hewn, explorer and made him second officer on the *Endurance*. He ended up being one of the men the Boss most liked and most trusted.

Shackleton chose a reliable deputy
who shared his views of leadership and was, above all, loyal.

One of Shackleton's first hires was the other "old dog" of the *Nimrod*, Frank Wild. No one could top Wild's experience in the Antarctic. Shackleton and Wild had met aboard the *Discovery*. Shackleton then put him in charge of stores on the *Nimrod*. Afterward, Wild joined Sir Douglas Mawson's scientific expedition to Adélie Land in Antarctica as head of one of the shore parties.

Shackleton saw real leadership potential in Frank Wild, the only man to serve on all three of the expeditions led by the Boss. During the desperate dash back to the *Nimrod*, it was Wild and not the second in command, Lt. J. B. Adams, who was at Shackleton's side. Shackleton found in Wild everything he needed in a No. 2: loyalty, cheerfulness, decency, strength, and experience. He was the same age as Shackleton and just as tough, although he had the opposite build: small and wiry. He had been in the merchant service and the Royal Navy, and so was familiar with the two cultures of British exploration.

Wild's job was to help select crew members, then continue working with them aboard ship to arrange daily routines and act as the liaison between them and the Boss. He handled all the men's gripes and their need for advice. He knew how to deal with all types, and inevitably earned the men's confidence and loyalty. Thomas Orde-Lees said of Wild on the *Endurance*: "Wild is our second in command and quite the most popular man (save our leader) amongst us. He has rare tact and the happy knack of saying nothing and yet getting people to do things just as he requires them. He acts as Sir Ernest's lieutenant and if he has any orders to give us he gives them in the nicest way, especially if it is instructions to carry out some particularly nasty work, such as 'trimming' coal in the bunkers or scrubbing the floor."

Wild was the son of a schoolteacher. He was clever but not an idea man, and he knew it. He left the thinking to Shackleton, to whom he was utterly devoted. He was, in other words, a perfect complement to Shackleton. His unpublished memoirs are a heartfelt account of his life with his mentor and show real insight into the dynamics of Shackleton's leadership. He became such a good student of Shackleton's strategy that he could step in for the Boss whenever necessary and Shackleton had complete confidence in him.

Shackleton wanted people who shared his vision and enthusiasm for exploration.

Shackleton made a mistake on the *Nimrod* by hiring individuals who didn't fit the bold, risk-taking culture of exploration. The two captains on the *Nimrod* appeared to be well qualified, but ultimately were not up to the unique challenges of the Antarctic. Shackleton had met the *Nimrod*'s first captain, Rupert England, four years earlier on Scott's relief ship, the *Morning*, where he was serving as first officer. But England turned out to be an overly cautious captain in the face of the brutal, unpredictable weather and was constantly shifting the ship's position, wasting precious fuel. He insisted on a coal supply for the ship's return that was nearly 40 percent over need, forcing the shore party to skimp on their share of the coal during the harsh winter. For the retrieval of the shore party after winter, Capt. England was replaced by Capt. Frederick Pryce Evans, who was even worse. He was the jittery captain who departed ahead of schedule, leaving Shackleton and his team behind.

For the *Endurance,* Shackleton wanted a captain with some bravado. Capt. Frank A. Worsley had it in spades. He was bold and a little eccentric—a "mad hat," Dr. Macklin of the *Endurance* called him. He was fond of a good story and a good joke, passing the Shackleton test for compatibility. He said he got the job after dreaming that he was sailing down London's Burlington Street past icebergs. The next morning, his story goes, he took a walk down that street, noticed the sign for the Imperial Trans-Antarctic Expedition, went in, and was hired.

The rest of the crew was selected in only a slightly more orthodox manner. Wild tore through the mountain of queries, quickly dismissing the vast majority of them. Sorting the telegrams, he'd drop them into one of three drawers he had marked "Mad," "Hopeless," and "Possible." The Possibles were shown to Shackleton. If the Boss approved, an interview was granted, after which Shackleton would make a decision. Those interviews were recounted by the men for years afterward.

Shackleton conducted
unconventional interviews to find unique talent.

Shackleton was a shrewd judge of character, and insisted on face-to-face meetings whenever possible in his business dealings. During first encounters with applicants, he held freewheeling exchanges that tended to be brief but intense. How candidates answered was more important than the content of their replies. The Boss was listening for enthusiasm and for subtle indications of their ability to be part of a team. As his biographer James Fisher observed, "It always looked as if he was picking them out with a pin but each time he got the right man." Observers called his methods "capricious" and "eccentric," but Shackleton was looking for extraordinary men to face the vast ice of the Antarctic. The traditional interview wouldn't have worked for the kind of mavericks he sought.

None of the applicants felt Shackleton was being frivolous. On the contrary, many were intimidated. Even those with the most outsized expectations of the explorer came away impressed. Dr. James A. McIlroy, hired as a surgeon on the *Endurance*, said the Boss "could be a very frightening kind of individual, like Napoleon; he was very stern looking and fixed you with a steely eye. I wasn't asked to sit down. I stood in front of him, facing the light. . . . He asked me lots of questions."

Reginald W. James, selected as *Endurance* physicist, described his peculiar interview: "Shackleton asked me if my teeth were good, if I suffered from varicose veins, if my circulation was good, if I had a good temper, and if I could sing. At this question I probably looked a bit taken aback, for I remember he said, 'Oh, I don't mean any Caruso stuff; but I suppose you can shout a bit with the boys?'"

The question about singing had become one of Shackleton's stock queries, and his touchstone for a man's team spirit. Raymond Priestley, who was named *Nimrod*'s geologist, wrote about a similar experience: "He asked me if I could sing and I said I couldn't; and he asked me if I would know gold if I saw it, and again I said No! He must have asked me other questions but I remember these because they were bizarre." Priestley was amazed he got the job without a university degree when "there were twelve people with honors degrees after the job." But Shackleton had seen something in him he liked. Priestley did, in fact, turn out to be a valuable and popular crew member.

The Boss liked optimists.
He saw them as the most likely team players.

Shackleton wanted men who contributed to esprit de corps, those with passion for the life of an explorer and confidence in success. One thing Shackleton looked for was a happy person. He told *Endurance* meteorologist Leonard Hussey, "Loyalty comes easier to a cheerful person than to one who carries a heavy countenance."

During Hussey's interview, the Boss constantly paced the office, seeming not to listen to the slight young man but clearly concentrating. "In a few minutes he must have sized me up," Hussey wrote.

"'You'll do, Hussey,' he said. 'I'll take you.'"

Hussey said the Boss told him later why he was selected: "I thought you looked funny!" He was right. Hussey, the smallest member of the *Endurance* crew, was "intensely funny," as a fellow crew member described him, and a good banjo player. His talent for entertaining would prove invaluable during the dark days after the men lost the *Endurance* and were struggling to keep their spirits up.

Of course, personality alone didn't guarantee a place in Shackleton's good graces. It had to accompany real talent. In Hussey's case, Shackleton was impressed that he had applied from Sudan, where he was part of another expedition. It showed a love of exploration and investigation that encompassed the globe. Hussey said Shackleton was "greatly amused to find amongst the five thousand applications to join the expedition, one that came from the heart of Africa."

Shackleton sought men
who really wanted the job.

The Boss rarely went begging. He put all his heart and soul into his work and he wanted men who would do the same. He saw that the candidates hungriest to be hired usually proved their mettle on the job. He recalled how he hired George Marston as ship artist for the *Nimrod* expedition. He had whittled a pile of thirty applicants down to three and sent telegrams to each on a Friday afternoon asking them to meet him in his office at a specific time the next day.

That Saturday, Shackleton made his way to the office in a downpour and found a note from one of the candidates. It said he was going out of town and asked to switch the appointment to Monday.

The second had written to say he would only make the four-hour trip to the office from his home if it were certain he would get the job. Shackleton hadn't heard from the third candidate, and was preparing to leave the office when a man, disheveled and soaking wet from the rain, rushed up. He told Shackleton that he had been on a walking tour in Cornwall when the telegram had been forwarded to his lodgings. He had immediately set out for London, taking several trains to get there.

"I promptly engaged him," Shackleton wrote. "I thought that if a man could be as quick as that in order to get a position, he was the man for it; and, as it turned out, my opinion was more than justified."

Marston was hired again for the *Endurance* expedition.

Shackleton needed hard workers
who wouldn't flinch at menial tasks.

Shackleton tried to weed out prima donnas who wanted the glamour of expedition celebrity without doing all the work involved. He needed men who worked as hard as he did, jacks-of-all-trades without airs. He didn't care what position the man held in society.

There were no passengers on board the *Endurance*. Everybody more or less mucked in. "It didn't matter who they were or what they were; their qualifications didn't count for anything," the seaman Walter How remembered. "The doctors used to take their turn at the wheel, they'd give a hand in the galley, they'd go aloft and take in sail and they'd set sail from the deck. Everybody was a utility firm, as it were."

On his last voyage in 1921, Shackleton had three open positions when he got to South America. About one hundred volunteered, including Christopher Naisbitt, who had asked an officer from the British Club in Brazil to introduce him to Shackleton. Shackleton took one look at the man dressed in "a Palm Beach suit and a Panama hat" and asked if he had ever worked hard a day in his life.

"I said I had served in the navy four years and was fond of sport," Naisbitt recalled. Shackleton asked if he knew he'd have to carry food from the galley on a rolling ship while drenched with sea water.

"I told him I was sure I could do the job," Naisbitt said. Shackleton tried to discourage him from joining the expedition, and when he couldn't, he suggested Naisbitt have a one-day trial. The Boss, who occasionally liked to try out prospective candidates, had him hauling supplies, peeling potatoes, swabbing the kitchen. He did the dirty work without complaint. Shackleton hired him.

Shackleton recruited those
who had the expertise he lacked.

Shackleton had little interest in science, but knew it was the bread and butter of exploration work. Accordingly, he recruited men like Reginald W. James, a talented physicist at Cambridge University, and Robert S. Clark, a biologist who had worked up the results of an earlier expedition to the Weddell Sea. Shackleton wasn't at all intimidated by their superior education and expertise. He even encouraged them to pursue their own projects on the expedition.

Far from distancing himself from scientific fieldwork in which he had no particular interest or ability, the Boss made an effort to familiarize himself with the experiments once the expedition got under way. Macklin marveled: "I have always regarded as one of the most remarkable traits of this remarkable man his ability to obtain a practical grasp of scientific and technical matters in regard to which he had no training."

Just before the *Endurance* voyage, another talent caught Shackleton's eye. He had gone to the cinema to see a remarkable example of the new genre of adventure documentary so popular at the time. *Home of the Blizzard* showed riveting footage of Douglas Mawson's 1912 expedition to the Antarctic. It was filmed by a twenty-six-year old Australian photographer named James Francis "Frank" Hurley. Shackleton knew Hurley's work would be highly prized and hired him sight unseen—a rare departure from his usual insistence on meeting in person. Wild was able to vouch for Hurley, having worked with him on Mawson's expedition.

It proved a wise choice. Not only was Hurley a gifted photographer, he was also "full of good suggestions," Shackleton would later write. Some of his shipmates considered Hurley a braggart, but he was tough, clever, and inventive. Trained as a metal worker, his skill would be put to use turning remnants of the crushed *Endurance* into useful items, such as a stove.

The Boss also saw potential in Thomas Orde-Lees, who rode to the interview on a motorcycle to show off his knowledge of new engines. In a show of support for the expedition, Orde-Lees was lent by the Royal Marines. He was hired to oversee the expedition's motorized sledges, which were more practical replacements for the car Shackleton had hauled along on the *Nimrod*.

Shackleton made sure every man
he hired knew exactly what was expected of him.

Shackleton took pains never to mislead with false promises. Macklin recalled, for example, that Shackleton made it clear to each that a man's standing with the party depended ultimately on whether he helped with all the general work aboard ship, in addition to his regular assignments.

He wrote letters to recruits, stating exactly what their duties and pay would be and what he wanted in return. The letters were also an opportunity to establish a personal connection, a habit Shackleton reinforced continually.

The Boss sent the following letter to Robert S. Clark on July 1, 1914, after he was hired as ship biologist:

The Imperial Trans-Antarctic Expedition

4, New Burlington Street
Regent Street
London, W.
1st July 1914

R. S. Clark Esq.,
Marine Biological Association of
the United Kingdom,
Plymouth.

Dear Sir,

I regret that great pressure of work has prevented me up to now making out a memorandum of our conversation.

I am in receipt of your letter of the 28th June and note contents. I now give the following statement of what I am prepared to offer you, but before doing so I note your remarks as regards leave of absence for one year only. We must get over this difficulty in some way, for one year is not sufficient, and I will refer to this matter in the course of the letter.

1.   Your salary will be £400 per annum (all clothing etc. provided by the Expedition) from the time you join the Expedition until the Expedition returns to England, or a period not more than two years. On the return of the Expedition you would attend to the working out of the biological results at a salary of £250 per annum, which work would be done in conjunction with your own duties in the laboratory. I note re the question of salary that you are willing to accept remuneration commensurate with the work to be done. I make always a standing salary and I expect all the work that it is possible for a man to do.

2.   I note you lay particular stress on a guarantee that funds will be forthcoming for the working out of the results of the

Expedition. I am prepared to have the results worked out and I have funds for that, but I make no guarantee to any man as regards such a matter. It is obvious that unless the results were worked out it is useless taking a biologist.

3.   You will be permanently attached to the ship "Endurance" and every facility given to you for biological work in the Antarctic seas and in other places.

4.   I am providing equipment for trawling up to 500 fathoms and I am prepared to provide whatever equipment you consider necessary for the work both on the ship and on the shore.

5.   I propose to have an assistant Biologist on board the ship who would work under you and the whole of the biological work of both Ross sea ship and base, and the Weddell sea ship and base will be under your direction and the collections in your charge.

6.   You will have every facility given to you for biological work compatible with the safety and necessary navigation of the "Endurance."

7.   You will sign on the articles of "Endurance" at 1s. [shilling] a month for the purpose of discipline, in that whilst a member of the Expedition you will be subject to the Captain's orders, but the Captain of the Ship will have my instructions to afford you every facility for your work. I might add in connection with this that Captain Worsley is himself very anxious to make a hydrographical and biological record on this expedition and is keenly interested in the subject.

8.   Regarding the question of leave of absence, I will if you think it advisable approach Prof. Shipley personally to get his goodwill for a longer leave, and I am further prepared to pay £200 a year for a man to temporarily take some of your work in the laboratory whilst you are engaged in this Expedition. I presume that the higher work could be delegated to var-

---

ious heads and the £200 a year man could do much to relieve them.

I would like to hear at your earliest convenience whether these terms are acceptable for I want to get the equipment ready now. I have already ordered, and am having installed, a Steam Winch for trawling and have ordered 1,500 fathoms of 1½" wire.

I have a Biological Laboratory arranged on the ship, but the fitting up and equipment of this I am leaving for the Biologist to attend to.

Believe me, dear Sir,

Yours faithfully,

(signature E. H. Shackleton)

P.S. I enclose cheque for £4 for your travelling expenses (initialed)

In general, Shackleton strove to make things easy for the crew. He knew, for example, that many of the men would be returning to their regular jobs after the voyage. For that reason, he offered to speak to their bosses to smooth things over or to help hire a temporary replacement. He also paid extra for more experienced men and sometimes added extra provisions for families as a kind of insurance against accidental death. Oddly, he failed to make prudent provisions for his own family. His wife, Emily, had to live off her own money after her husband's death.

Shackleton equipped the crew with state-of-the-art tools.

Though perpetually strapped for funds, Shackleton invested in the finest quality equipment. He had concluded that shoddy tools wasted time and money. Perhaps he never forgot how he suffered as an apprentice from his employer's refusal to use the latest devices to help load and unload the ship. In the Antarctic, cutting corners like that could threaten lives. Everything for the *Endurance* was the best available at that time: sledges, skis, axes, ropes, tools, electric lighting, even diaries and toothpaste.

Orde-Lees wrote about the *Endurance* expedition that "every regard was made to the protection of life and limb and the general health of the party, unlimited attention was given to the all important matter of diet and the polar equipment and scientific instruments were all of the latest type and well nigh perfect; in fact nothing was left to chance except the ice, a factor which no amount of provision could regulate."

Shackleton divided up the work of outfitting the *Endurance* allowing the men who were using the equipment to help make purchasing decisions. Shackleton handled the ship, its fittings, and the dogs; Wild took care of provisions; Marston saw to clothing, tents, bedding, and dog harnesses; Marston and Wild both helped with sledges, skis, and huts; Orde-Lees handled machinery and tools; and the doctors and scientists evaluated the instruments and medical supplies.

The crewmen were issued Burberry boots based on a design by Amundsen for use with five pairs of socks. (As it turned out, the uppers were prone to leak.) They also brought finneskos, literally "Finnish shoes"—boots made of reindeer skins, with a moisture-absorbing type of grass inside. On the rough ice, they wore out quickly so each man in the shore party was issued multiple pairs. They had balaclava helmets that covered their ears, and state-of-the-art snow goggles tinted with greenish yellow to prevent snow blindness. For use on the overland trek, Shackleton borrowed some scientific instruments from the Royal Geographical Society and the Admiralty, and bought the rest. As was customary, the *Endurance* also received gifts from friends and manufacturers. They had a special thin-paper edition of the *Encyclopaedia Britannica*. One friend donated a private library of polar books, later lost in the disaster—except for a couple of volumes secretly saved by two of the crewmen as a gesture of gratitude. Scott's photographer, the renowned Herbert Ponting, sent cake and wine, and Emily Shackleton gave the men homemade sweets.

Like all explorers, Shackleton was an inveterate inventor, ceaselessly searching for the tiniest improvements and innovations in the logistics and methods of mounting a complex expedition. Indeed, some of his most important contributions to the field were in this realm. The Boss, for example, improved upon Norwegian explorer Fridtjof Nansen's fur clothing, replacing the heavy, cumbersome material with lighter windproof Burberry gabardine suits.

With his merchant-marine background, packing was a particular Shackleton forte. In his experience, expedition leaders often gave far too little attention to this area, carrying equipment in whatever container the manufacturer had provided. Scott had used some custom-made cases fashioned from Venesta, an early plywood made of three layers of wood glued together; but they came in various sizes and shapes. For the *Nimrod,* Shackleton ordered twenty-five hundred Venesta packing cases in a uniform size. This not only made packing easier, but after the boxes were emptied they could be used to build partitions and furniture for the hut. Shackleton figured he had saved four tons of weight by not having to carry furnishings on board. The hut for the *Endurance* expedition was to be constructed of fir timbers and layers of matchboard, with double doors and windows to keep out the cold. Marston also cleverly designed two types of hoop tents that could be set up quickly in a blizzard and that were roomier than tents used on previous expeditions.

Shackleton took the greatest care with food supplies. He believed that a varied diet was a key to good health and good spirits. The worst suffering on prior expeditions had stemmed from bringing the wrong food, having too little of it, and spoilage. On his first trip South, Shackleton himself had developed scurvy—caused by a lack of vitamin C—and suffered swollen limbs and gums, among other symptoms. Upon his return, he studied the disease and how to prevent it, becoming more knowledgeable than most medical experts of his day. Even with the serious food shortage suffered by *Nimrod*'s Farthest South party, no one developed scurvy because they were eating fresh meat from the ponies.

The *Endurance* was able to stock two years' worth of food by using the most advanced packaging methods of the day. Some items were hermetically sealed. Soups were highly concentrated. Vegetables were dried and compressed into three-inch square tins. Realizing that the British military faced a similar challenge in feeding constantly moving groups, Shackleton sent Frank Wild to consult with Major General Sir Wilfred Beveridge at the War Office. They calculated the number of calories required by marching men (about four thousand a day), and came up with a nutritious diet suitable for men having to march in a polar climate.

Some thought Shackleton tended to overdo his menus. Douglas Mawson, the Australian explorer, took home from the *Nimrod* a huge block of chocolate and for years afterward when anyone visited his office at Adelaide University, he took an ice ax and hacked off a chunk to offer them. The *Nimrod* left behind such sumptuous provisions that when a party from Scott's *Terra Nova* expedition of 1910–1913 made it to Shackleton's Cape Royds hut they were treated to biscuits that puffed up when heated, jars of fruit, boiled chicken, kidney, mushrooms, ginger mutton cutlets, and candied orange peel.

To pay for it all, Shackleton had to do extensive fundraising. For the *Nimrod* expedition, which cost about £30,000 ($6 million in today's dollars), he relied on credit and went into huge debt. For the *Endurance*, which cost about £50,000 (about $10 million in today's currency), he took the very modern step of preselling the rights to stories, photographs, and film. The *Endurance* budget was little more than half what the publicly funded *Discovery* had been thirteen years earlier.

Shackleton sent an elaborate prospectus, with a personal letter attached, to several hundred potential backers. The joke was that some of England's wealthy industrialists were all too happy to help send Shackleton to the bottom of the earth in order to get him away from their wives. Shackleton was linked to several women, among them a stage actress named Rosalind Chetwynd. Certainly, many society matrons were swayed by his charms, but it isn't clear that he was a philanderer of the magnitude many have claimed him to be.

Shackleton's exhausting and often frustrating fundraising effort ultimately bore fruit. At the eleventh hour, a major benefactor stepped forward with a generous gift of £24,000 to get the *Endurance* expedition under way. He was Sir James Caird, a Scottish jute manufacturer and philanthropist who was fond of travel. He gave the money with no strings attached, and made an open appeal to other donors not to ask for repayment. Caird's generosity won him a slice of immortality: His name was given to the lifeboat that carried Shackleton on his voyage across the South Atlantic to get help for his stranded men. The other two lifeboats made famous in the *Endurance* saga were named for Janet Stancomb-Wills, a British tobacco heiress, and Dudley Docker, a British industrialist. The government's contribution was a modest £10,000, and another £1,000 came from the Royal Geographical Society.

Wild and Shackleton mostly finished hiring the expedition by the early summer of 1914. They had to make some last-minute replacements, ending up with some men who were not carefully screened. The threat of war in Europe was siphoning off some of the most qualified men and creating problems with the delivery of goods. In the end, however, the *Endurance* was a well-fitted, well-staffed expedition.

Circumstances would test these men in ways they never expected. But they would pull together for nearly two years and bring themselves to safety. Frank Wild was unflappable and could carry on when Shackleton had to separate from the crew. Seaman

Timothy McCarthy managed to be cheerful at times when others feared losing their sanity. Frank Worsley was a brilliant navigator. Tom Crean helped rescue the crew during the most difficult leg of the journey. Louis Rickinson was inexhaustible. The surgeons, Drs. Alexander H. Macklin and James A. McIlroy, were both level-headed and versatile. Photographer Frank Hurley was to do the best work of his life.

The *Endurance* set sail on Saturday, August 1, 1914. She left the West India Dock under the bright sun of summer and the dark cloud of the beginning of World War I. The expedition was given a noisy send-off by a crowd of cheering people standing at the docks, by a chorus of ships' sirens, and by a bagpiper who played "The Wearin' o' the Green." The ship sailed down the Thames.

That Monday, Shackleton was crestfallen when he went ashore in Margate, England, and read news of a call for a general mobilization. Several officers left immediately. Shackleton returned to the ship and asked his men for their permission to place the ship at the disposal of the Admiralty. An hour after sending a telegram, he got the reply: "Proceed." Shortly afterward, another telegram came from First Lord of the Admiralty Winston Churchill insisting there was no need to interrupt plans made by "the highest geographical authorities." The king personally offered his best wishes for the expedition. Shackleton, at last, felt he could send the ship off with a clear conscience. The following Saturday, the *Endurance* entered the open seas.

Shackleton, Wild, and two of the scientists stayed behind to make final arrangements and to wait for some essential items that had not been delivered on time. Finally, Shackleton left Liverpool on September 25 and headed to Buenos Aires, where he would join the *Endurance*. By then, he was tired, nervous, and worried. He wrote a contrite letter to his wife that showed his deep conflicts over sacrificing family for work and his willingness to make the promise he never kept: "I am just obsessed with my work and all I have to do . . . I am going to carry through this work and then there will be an end, I expect, to my wanderings for any length of time in far places."

In the two months it took to reach Argentina, many of the crew (mostly the professionals and scientists) found themselves homesick, seasick, fearful, and not at all convinced they had made the right decision. Those who weren't discontent (mostly the seamen) were having a rip-roaring time drinking, carousing, and running afoul of the law in port. All of this goes to prove that even the most capable crew still needs a good leader.

Orde-Lees began complaining on his first day at sea: "I am beginning to funk it as usual & wish I had not come. I don't see the use of Polar exploration at all," he wrote in his diary. His despair grew as the weeks wore on, as several members of the crew became increasingly rowdy without the steadying hand of Shackleton at the helm. In October 1914, Orde-Lees made another entry: "The crew, or at least 10 out of 12 are behaving most disloyally, going out every day on the drink and leaving us, the staff, to do all the work. This shows something wrong somewhere, but it will all be put right when Sir Ernest arrives, thank goodness."

SHACKLETON'S WAY OF
SELECTING AND ORGANIZING A CREW

- Start with a solid core of workers you know from past jobs or who come recommended by trusted colleagues.

- Your No. 2 is your most important hire. Pick one who complements your management style, shows loyalty without being a yes-man, and has a talent for working with others.

- Hire those who share your vision. Someone who clashes with your personality or the corporate culture will hinder your work.

- Be a creative, unconventional interviewer if you seek creative, unconventional people. Go deeper than job experience and expertise. Ask questions that reveal a candidate's personality, values, and perspective on work and life.

- Surround yourself with cheerful, optimistic people. They will reward you with the loyalty and camaraderie vital for success.

- Applicants hungriest for the job are apt to work hardest to keep it.

- To weed out potential slackers, choose workers who show a willingness to tackle any job, and will take a turn at the unpopular tasks.

- Hire those with the talents and expertise you lack. Don't feel threatened by them. They will help you stay on the cutting edge and bring distinction to your organization.

- Spell out clearly to new employees the exact duties and requirements of their jobs, and how they will be compensated. Many failed work relationships start with a lack of communication.

- To help your staff do top-notch work, give them the best equipment you can afford. Working with outdated, unreliable tools creates an unnecessary burden.

WORKING IT IN

James J. Cramer credits Shackleton's optimistic example with nothing less than rescuing him from financial ruin and relative obscurity just months before he gained success, personal wealth, and international fame as a major player on Wall Street.

"Shackleton saved my life," he says simply.

Mr. Cramer read about Shackleton in late 1998, at the end of the worst year of his professional life. His New York-based hedge fund Cramer Berkowitz & Company was in its deepest slump since its launch in 1987. A tumbling stock market in the second half of the year caused the aggressive fund to lose $100 million and finish the year with just a 2 percent return on assets. "People were pulling out capital," Mr. Cramer recalls. "I personally lost $15 million. It was time to hunker down."

He was also having headaches at his fledgling financial-news Web site, TheStreet.com, which he cofounded in 1996 with Martin Peretz, owner and editor of *The New Republic*. In 1998, the company's losses widened dramatically to $16.4 million from $5.8 million the previous year, even though revenue had surged past the million-dollar mark.

It came to the point where Mr. Cramer had to ask himself and his backers, "Are we knocked out?" He called his partners and found a level of pessimism that surprised and overwhelmed him. They told him to fold. He felt defeated. "You drag yourself to work every morning, but you're down and people are laughing at you," he says, recalling the torture of having to face staff and colleagues at his Wall Street office every day.

Then he found Shackleton.

After seeing an article about the explorer in *National Geographic,* Mr. Cramer read *Endurance* by Alfred Lansing and then Shackleton's account of the same expedition, *South.* "I felt like this really was the philosophy—for life, too, but for business especially," he says.

Amid all the voices telling him to give up, he heard Shackleton telling him to stick with it. He started writing quotations from Shackleton in red marker on the white board in his office to bolster his and his staff's spirits. "Optimism is true moral courage," stayed up through the entire 1998 sell-off, Mr. Cramer says.

"If I hadn't been schooled by Shackleton, I would have given up," he says. "It was the worst year I ever had. He got me through it because everybody, everybody tells you to give up. But I came back in a style that was unbelievable and proved the pessimists were wrong."

Wrong indeed. By early 1999, his interests had made a dramatic turnaround, and he was catapulted into fame and a good deal of fortune. The New York Times Company and Rupert Murdoch's News Corporation took minority stakes in TheStreet.com and eventually set up joint ventures. His hedge fund, which had tumbled to about $180 million in assets in 1998, more than doubled in value.

The big payoff came in May 1999, when TheStreet.com went public. Mr. Cramer's Shackleton-like media savvy and gift for gab had created such a buzz about the company that demand for its shares swamped the Nasdaq Stock Market. Trading of the shares was delayed until two hours after opening. When the stock was finally offered, the price per share surged to $73, almost four times the $19 initial offering price, and then settled at $60 for the close. About 13.5 million shares of TheStreet.com were traded that day. Based on the initial closing price, total market capitalization for the company was estimated at $1.42 billion. That meant the forty-four-year-old Mr. Cramer's stake in the company was valued at more than $215 million—at a time when his annual salary was $250,000.

The company drew international attention. Subscriptions and visits to the site surged, more staff was added, and the company moved into bigger quarters. (Mr. Cramer, as a trader and a market commentator, must maintain a cautious distance from activities of TheStreet.com and doesn't work from its offices.) Never mind that the company was never profitable; revenue in 1999 more than tripled. The bottom line was irrelevant for pioneer Internet concerns, market bulls reasoned. "TheStreet.com represents the future," said *USA Today*. Credit for the success went to Mr. Cramer, whom the paper described as having "the look of an overcaffeinated poster boy for the Type A set."

Mr. Cramer's cheerful face, sporting a red goatee, could be seen everywhere after that, prompting *The Wall Street Journal* to call him "a Wall Street lightning rod for attention and publicity." He appeared on network television and on cable news shows. In addition to writing his own online columns—brazenly called "Wrong!"—he turned out articles for other magazines and newspapers and forged alliances with numerous media and corporate outlets. His enormous popularity prompted *Talk* magazine to name him one of the fifty Americans people listened to in 1999.

Mr. Cramer's commentary is brashly in-your-face. He rants about outmoded concepts in finance and teases the "dead-tree boys" in the print media. With characteristic chutzpah, he declares TheStreet.com is "the people's choice."

In one year, Mr. Cramer had made a stellar comeback from the brink. "There was such unbelievable pressure to give up and call it quits," he recalls. Had he done so, he says now, "It would have been the dumbest decision of my life."

Mr. Cramer, a Harvard graduate, served as president of *The Harvard Crimson* before going on to get a law degree from the university. He worked for a time as a journalist and helped found *Smart Money* magazine. He had a stint in the private-client-services unit of Goldman Sachs & Company before he launched Cramer & Company in 1987 with his wife, Karen. He was joined about four years later by Jeff Berkowitz.

Today, Mr. Cramer, who has an interest in history, has a photograph of Sir Ernest in his office, with a note in Shackleton's handwriting dated to the *Nimrod* expedition that he bought at auction.

When he hires people now, Mr. Cramer thinks of how Shackleton analyzed his crew. He chooses optimists, he says, and those who share his ideas and hopes for his business. He concedes he's still striving to more fully emulate the explorer. "I wish I could be a little more like him," he laments. "People respected him in his position in a way I could only dream of. There was a respectful distance between him and his men. I'm too buddy-buddy."

As the new century dawned, some of the sizzle had gone out of Internet stocks and TheStreet.com was again being battered. One year after the red-hot IPO, the company had gone through a shake-up of top management, the stock had fallen to below its opening price, and the site had become mostly free of charge. Mr. Cramer gave up his salary in favor of stock options, and there were rumors of a pending sale.

He continued to ignore the naysayers, however, insisting that those working hard toward a goal must stay optimistic. "If you surround yourself with pessimists you're doomed to failure in business," Mr. Cramer says. "They are the voices you can't let in your head. If you listen to the pessimists you'll make the wrong decision or be so confused and so befuddled you'll lose the emotional energy you need."

3

CREATING A SPIRIT
OF CAMARADERIE

Any and every duty is undertaken cheerfully and willingly and no complaint or whining is ever heard no matter what hardships or inconvenience may be encountered. The principal credit of this is due to the tact and leadership of the head of the expedition and the cheery happiness and bonhomie of Wild. They both command respect, confidence and affection.

—Frank Worsley, captain, *Endurance*

CREW CUT

The men of the *Endurance* had the sudden urge to shave their heads one afternoon, giving them the look of "a cargo of convicts," as one described it.
The Boss encouraged the group to work and play together to build camaraderie and keep up an air of conviviality. They performed skits, held sing-
alongs, celebrated birthdays, and every Saturday night held the traditional
seamen's toast to "Sweethearts and Wives."

SHACKLETON DID SET THINGS STRAIGHT ON THE SHIP, BUT EVEN Thomas Orde-Lees couldn't have predicted how great a difference his leadership would make. As good as Shackleton was at selecting talented men, he was better at leading them. He could afford to hire on the basis of personality and character because he knew he could get above-average performances out of even the most average of men.

At the start of the *Nimrod* expedition in 1907, an inexperienced Shackleton bragged to his wife about his "perfect" crew and provisions. He ended up disappointed in some key people, clashed with others, and was imperiled by miscalculations in needed supplies. By the time the *Endurance* sailed in 1914, Shackleton was forty years old and an experienced leader. He no longer had illusions about the perfection of men or supplies; he knew that the Ice could destroy either, and that the ultimate success or failure of the venture rested with him. He had matured into a more confident, shrewder, and much more decisive leader. He had learned from his earliest years at sea what he hated most about his jobs—pettiness, irresponsible bosses, insufferable working conditions, and a lack of trust and respect among crew members. As a rookie expedition leader, he had learned what didn't work—leadership that was rigid, remote, undemocratic, and uncertain. On the *Endurance,* he focused on the one thing that gave him the best chance at reaching his goals: unity.

"There are lots of good things in the world, but I'm not sure that comradeship is not the best of them all," *Endurance* meteorologist Leonard Hussey remembered Shackleton saying.

Building a united and loyal crew was the foundation of Shackleton's leadership. For the Boss, teamwork was more than an ingredient for success; it was a goal in itself. He always loved his crew even if he didn't always love all its members, and he relished the task of building a bond among them and with them. "Adventure is the soul of existence because it [brings] out true harmony among men," Shackleton told Hussey.

Pulling the *Endurance* crew together would not be easy. The group was divided by social class, occupation, and temperament. They had been hired from around the English-speaking world and had come together in Argentina from various early assignments. Frank Wild, geologist James Wordie, and physicist Reginald James arrived in Buenos Aires separately with the sledge dogs. Photographer Frank Hurley came in from Australia. The initial separation created cliques that had to be broken down. But even the crew that took the *Endurance* across the Atlantic on the first leg of the journey was fractured. The professionals felt superior to the seamen. The seamen felt superior to the wimpy college boys.

What's more, with Capt. Frank Worsley in charge, the men grew inured to conflict and lack of discipline. Many resented the work they had to do and only managed the minimum. Those who did try to carry their own weight felt unappreciated. Instead of rewarding their participation, Worsley and ship officers Hubert Hudson and Lionel Greenstreet responded with arrogance. "They threw their weight about and tended to treat the scientific staff as quite inferior beings," Dr. Alexander Macklin commented in 1957.

That changed with the arrival of Shackleton.

New on the scene, Shackleton observed before he
acted, only making changes to make improvements.

The Boss arrived in Buenos Aires on Friday, October 16, about six weeks after the *Endurance* had anchored. Still, he didn't board the ship for several days, choosing instead to stay in the Palace Hotel while he assessed the problems inside and outside the ship. Shackleton never made arbitrary decisions just to prove he was in charge.

One immediate problem was that the ship was being held up by red tape at the port. Sir Ernest went to the highest authority and broke the stalemate. Biographer H. R. Mill wrote humorously that Shackleton, who had successfully charmed "cold-blooded businessmen" in England into parting with their money, had little trouble dealing with the more agreeable Argentine officials: "All doors opened, all wheels ran smoothly, everything was done, done quickly, and with an air of Castilian grace."

Shackleton used less charm in setting things right with the crew. He dismissed some of them and hired replacements in port. Experience had taught him to be less tentative about weeding out those who weren't up to the job. He had made no changes on the *Nimrod* after leaving England; on the *Endurance* he fired four; and on his last voyage, the *Quest,* he was hiring and firing all the way to South America.

One of Shackleton's first moves in Buenos Aires was to fire the *Endurance*'s incompetent cook—no surprise considering the huge importance Shackleton placed on food. The replacement was Charles Green, an eccentric baker with a high-pitched voice that the men loved to mock. Green proved to be a phenomenon, able to whip up huge, hot meals while clinging to ice-covered rocks during gales. Shackleton would later single him out as one of the heroes of the expedition.

At the same time, he signed on an American seaman, William Bakewell, who had identified himself as a Canadian in order to qualify as a British subject for the expedition. A couple of days

later, Shackleton fired two seamen for being absent without permission for a week. The next day another was let go. The Boss bent
rules to his liking all the time, but he still believed in rules. He over-
looked plenty of the reported shenanigans in port, but would not
tolerate a lack of commitment. Still, Shackleton didn't leave the
fired men stranded in South America. He helped them find jobs on
a steamer headed back to England.

Shackleton made himself accessible to his crew, listened to his
men's concerns, and kept them informed about the ship's business.

Shackleton was extremely busy during his time in Buenos Aires,
but his door was always open to the crewmen. Orde-Lees wrote
about how pleased he was to be welcomed into the Boss's hotel
quarters in Buenos Aires after church one Sunday for coffee.
Shackleton answered all the questions his motor expert had about
plans for the journey and got from him a sense of how the crew had
fared on the voyage. "He certainly endears himself to me more and
more every time I meet him," Orde-Lees wrote in his diary.

It had been the same with the *Nimrod* crew. Lt. J. B. Adams, second in command, noted that in the winter hut set up on the Antarctic coast during that expedition, any request for a change in policy
was always discussed with those who were affected.

When Shackleton did finally go aboard the *Endurance,* his cabin
served as a sort of safe haven where crew members could speak to
him out of earshot of the others, or go to convalesce. The Boss initially shared the space with Capt. Worsley, to get to know him better and to influence and acculturate him. When the crew later
moved to a warmer part of the ship, Shackleton stayed behind in
his cabin. This separation helped him maintain a respectful distance
from the rest of the men and gave him privacy to think and write.

The *Endurance* set sail from Argentina to South Georgia in the
South Atlantic on October 27. Two days out to sea, a young stowaway appeared: Perce Blackborow, a friend of the new American
seaman Bakewell. He had hidden in a locker. "I think he liked the

idea," ship artist George Marston said of Shackleton's reaction. Apparently, Shackleton figured someone with the guts to stow away might be an asset. And because he was a couple of hands short, he gave the nineteen-year-old a tryout until the ship reached South Georgia. By the time the *Endurance* arrived at the island two weeks later, the Boss decided he liked the young man very much. Finally, the crew was complete.

At this time, Shackleton sent letters home to Emily in which he again poured out his feelings about his life's calling and his family. "It seems a hard thing to say but this I know is my Ishmaelite life and the one thing that I am suited for, and in which I yield to no one. . . . I am just good as an explorer and nothing else," he wrote in one of them. In a later letter, he added, "I am never going away for a long journey like this again. I want to see the whole family comfortably settled and then coil up my ropes and rest. I think nothing of the world and the public; they cheer you one minute and howl you down the next. It is what one is oneself and what one makes of one's life that matters."

The Boss also wrote to his wife that he was dissatisfied with a few unnamed members of the crew. Time would show that most of the problems were manageable: the arrogance of Frank Hurley, the inexperience of Reginald James, and the selfish laziness of Thomas Orde-Lees. After the ordeal, however, an exhausted Shackleton wrote another letter to Emily calling one man "a fool" and another "no good." Ultimately, he denied the Polar Medal for distinguished service to four: carpenter Harry McNeish, for his mutinous protest against Capt. Worsley at a crucial moment during their struggle; seaman John Vincent for apparently pilfering the valuables Shackleton once ordered everyone to discard; and, for reasons never entirely clear, seamen Ernest Holness and William Stephenson. After all those men went through, many see it as unduly harsh and unforgiving and incongruous to Shackleton's otherwise generous nature to deny them their individual reward. But it would have been stranger had Shackleton ignored behavior he considered out of line or putting the lives of others at risk. Shackleton judged his men's performance on two levels: doing the job well and proving loyalty. Loyalty was by far the more important.

Shackleton's letter to Emily also revealed misgivings about his ship. It had leaked during the trip from England, and "her way of behaving" at the dock in Buenos Aires suggested she wasn't as strong as his first ship. "I would exchange her for the old *Nimrod* any day except for comfort," he wrote.

The *Endurance,* crammed with men, provisions, dogs, and kennels, arrived at the Norwegian whaling station of Grytviken in South Georgia in early November. Shackleton was warned that the ice in the Weddell Sea was the worst in anyone's memory. He waited on the island for a month, hoping the conditions would improve as the southern hemisphere's summer progressed. The ship finally left for the Antarctic on December 5.

Shackleton established order and routine on board the ship in order to foster an atmosphere of security and productivity.

The Boss was a stickler for structuring the day, setting clear parameters for both work and leisure. The comfortable daily routine helped each member of the crew feel that his work contributed to the smooth operation of the ship. Shortly after Shackleton boarded the ship, Orde-Lees wrote in his diary: "It is splendid having Sir Ernest on board; everything works like clockwork and one knows just where one is."

The men were expected to clean their living quarters and do their own laundry. The simplest task took an enormous amount of time and effort: It took hours of stoking fires under icy water, for instance, to get enough water to fill a tub to wash clothes. But as Shackleton well knew, keeping the men continually occupied helped combat boredom.

The general routine was a simple one, and no one dared ignore it. "Breakfast was at 9 A.M. sharp else woe betide," wrote Hurley.

"Sir Ernest's humor in the morning before breakfast is very erratic."

The absence of an hour-by-hour regimen, as Shackleton had designed, had unhinged the crew under Capt. Worsley, who himself appreciated the improvement. "Certainly a good deal of our cheerfulness is due to the order and routine which Sir E. establishes where he settles down," the captain wrote later. "The regular daily task and matter-of-fact groove into which everything settles inspires confidence in itself, and the leader's state of mind is naturally reflected in the whole party."

Shackleton broke down the traditional hierarchies by having everyone pitch in to do all the work on the ship.

Shackleton had a unique way of balancing the work of the scientists and the seamen, or as he called them, "the A.B.s and the B.A.s," for able-bodied seamen and those with bachelor of arts degrees. He had the scientists share in the ship's chores, making them occasionally put aside their scientific work for more pressing duties. He also had the seamen help take scientific readings and samples. Even the cook had a newly trained backup. Part of Shackleton's strategy grew from his having to economize. It was also a rejection of any traditional seafaring hierarchies and had the salubrious effect of building a crew of generalists skilled in all aspects of the ship's operations. Long before it was an accepted ideal, Shackleton strove for a democratic crew. "When Shackleton took over control of the ship, the ship officers had to climb down a peg or two, and did not take kindly to the new scheme of things," Dr. Macklin said.

Everyone had to take his turn sailing and steering the ship and doing night watch, which entailed noting ice conditions, maintaining the fires in the furnaces, and taking meteorological readings. In addition, all hands had to share such tasks as scrubbing the common spaces, "trimming" the coal by leveling off the pile, packing and unpacking the provisions, and caring for the dogs. "You'd see them on their hands and knees scrubbing," Seaman Walter How explained. "Mr. Clark and Dr. Macklin, they'd all take their turn." No one complained, he said, and "if they did it was no good. There was one man [who was] boss there and what he said went."

On the *Nimrod* expedition, according to Frank Wild, a popular mess man always received a lot of help washing up, while the unpopular ones were left to labor alone. On the *Endurance,* Shackleton didn't leave such gestures to chance; he made sure everyone received the help he needed. Shackleton also got rid of an extra layer of supervision that he had had on the *Nimrod*. On that expedition, Prof. Edgeworth David supervised the scientists; on the *Endurance,* Shackleton put the scientists in charge of their own projects, and had each report directly to him.

The benefit and logic of Shackleton's demands made sense even to Orde-Lees, who had fought with Capt. Worsley over chores during the entire trip from England to South America. "So, I find we have got to work!" Thomas Orde-Lees wrote in his diary not long after leaving the British port. Orde-Lees was one of those workers who always thought orders were meant for the other guy. "I have the middle watch tonight, 12 to 4 A.M.," he continued. "We go to bed and only get up if required. We are generally roused but never really required as far as I can see. But all merchant service and naval officers can think of nothing else but their ship, and think everyone else ought to take the same amount of interest in the beastly ship. They are most inconsiderate people and have no respect for 'passengers' and their night's rest."

After Shackleton took over, Orde-Lees began to see things differently. "I must say that I think scrubbing floors is not fair work for people who have been brought up in refinement. On the other hand, I think that under the present circumstances it has a desirable purpose as a disciplinary measure; it humbles one and knocks out of one any last remnants of false pride that one may have left in one, and for this reason I do it voluntarily and without being asked, but always with mingled feelings of revulsion and self-abnegation."

The egalitarian division of work, which was instituted at the start of the voyage, was unusual enough to draw the attention of outsiders. Dr. Macklin describes pulling into Buenos Aires where they were guided into port by a local tug: "I was at the wheel when we entered, and the pilot was intensely amused that a doctor should be doing such work, saying that the Argentine doctors all get seasick the moment they set foot aboard ship. When we finally reached our berth he showed me off to all the bystanders as a great curiosity."

Everyone did not have exactly equal status, but each was valued equally and treated with equal respect.

Shackleton rotated work assignments so that over time, each man worked alongside all the others, blurring divisions.

The Boss's work rotation scheme fostered an air of impartiality and encouraged friendships. Frank Hurley took a telling picture aboard the *Endurance* that shows three of the men—James Wordie, Alfred Cheetham, and Dr. Macklin—down on all fours, with rags in their hands, working shoulder-to-shoulder and knee-to-knee, scrubbing the patterned linoleum floor of the main living area.

For important and lengthy assignments, such as forming teams to explore the interior of the continent, Shackleton grouped the men according to personality type and actual friendships. For other jobs, however, he mixed and matched the workers randomly. The cleaning and the night-watch duties, for example, were assigned in alphabetical order. As if in a kind of square dance, crewmen continually changed partners for various assignments. Soon, the men habitually helped each other without being ordered to by Shackleton. Capt. Worsley took hydrographic readings and helped train and exercise dogs for sledge teams. First Officer Greenstreet helped Clark, the geologist, and Hurley, the photographer, with their work. The scientists put up dog kennels and carried the stores on board.

The mixing of duties boosted everyone's confidence in their

competence. This in turn led to more mixing on a social level. One can see in their diaries how friendly all the men were toward each other. As the men's routines became second nature, so did the bonds between them, and the resulting trust and camaraderie served them well in the more difficult times ahead.

A diary entry of the often malcontent carpenter, McNeish, shows the effect of Shackleton's social engineering: "Myself, Dr. McIlroy and the chief engineer scrubbed out the [living quarters] as the three of us do every Wednesday and Saturday. Then, we went for a walk and got back in time for [dinner], as it was getting a bit dark."

The same kind of mixing was accomplished on the *Nimrod* expedition. "There was no need for any 'after' or 'fore' quarters, not only because the party was so small but also because class distinctions were not considered when it was designed," geologist Raymond Priestley wrote. "Not that these were not felt. The differences in the table manners of petty officers and scientists were duly noted—and laughed at. Once, a conversation about university education promised to become awkward—but didn't. The fact remained that on this expedition, what counted was a man's proficiency. Some were proficient with their hands, some with their heads, some (notably Shackleton) were both. The scientific staff, taking their turn with domestic chores, acquired a few unwanted domestic skills."

Shackleton was scrupulously
evenhanded in all his dealings with the crew.

Shackleton had strong opinions about his crewmen, but thanks to his equitable system of governing the ship, they generally remained hidden. Hurt feelings and slights were taken seriously by the Boss. In one incident, the seamen registered a complaint against the storekeeper, Orde-Lees. Although the cramped quarters meant the seamen had to eat apart from the rest of the crew (as did the cook and the stowaway), they were given the same rations as Shackleton and the officers. They represented 25 percent of the crew and so were guaranteed 25 percent of all provisions, even the luxury items.

As Orde-Lees related it:

> The sailors had ben hinting that they did not get their fair share of little luxuries, such as sauces, etc., for by their agreement they are on the same rations as we are. I had always taken scrupulous care to see that they did get fair treatment, and recently Sir Ernest ordered me to give them one quarter of the contents of every case of delicacies I opened. The next day, I opened a case of 24 bottles of Heinz's chutney, gave the bo'sun ½ doz. and asked him to initial the receipt of them in my issue book, or rather I gave the articles to another man and told him to give the bo'sun this.
>
> This man told the bo'sun that I wanted him to write out a receipt for the goods.
>
> This seemed to hurt his feelings and he complained to the chief officers and by the time it reached Sir Ernest it was said that I wanted each man to sign for each course of his dinner every day, or some exaggeration of that sort. This was unfortunate but I did not think it worth wasting Sir Ernest's time with useless explanations, especially as he was very nice about it, but he said that it was contrary to the spirit of the expedition and of the merchant service, but I could see that he was displeased and that he considered that I had made a blunder.
>
> It seems such a trifle, yet I would have given a lot for it not to have occurred. Of course, I cannot get out of "service" ways. In the "service" it would have been far more serious to have omitted to have obtained a receipt.

Shackleton never let the punishment exceed the crime. Dr. Macklin recalled one day when two of the men on watch tangled a wire rope in the ship's propeller. "It was a very nasty thing and a very nasty accident," he said, "but there was no recrimination at all.

The thing was done and the thing was to get it undone. And throughout the whole of my association with [Shackleton], that was one feature that I noticed."

Dr. Macklin said that anytime the Boss felt he had come down too hard on someone, he undid any bad effect with an intimate talk. "He immediately put you back on a feeling of righteousness with him," he said.

Shackleton led by example.
He never asked anyone to do work he wouldn't do himself.

Shackleton lent a hand with even the most menial tasks when he was needed. If anyone was ill or injured, he'd be the likely one to take his place. He helped with the heavy lifting, the cleaning, and even laid linoleum. "He had cleaned up the wardroom far better than the majority of night watchmen," Orde-Lees said.

Shackleton was a consistent presence in the work area. His participation had many advantages: It allowed him to show by example how he expected things to be done; it gave him a better understanding of the effort involved in each task; it helped him evaluate the strengths and weaknesses of each man; it gave a certain dignity to all the jobs on board; and it enhanced his standing with the crew. Most of all, it allowed him to bond with his men.

The Boss had done the same on the *Nimrod*. "In the long winter months, when the scientists toiled in darkness and cold at their routine tasks outside, the help and company of our leader might always be relied upon," said Priestley. "He was equally at home exercising ponies, digging trenches for the examination of lake or sea-ice, collecting geological specimens, taking the place of an ailing biologist on the dredging line, assisting at a trial run of the motor car, or breaking in a team of dogs."

As the ice conditions worsened for the *Endurance*, Shackleton's helpfulness made the men feel more at ease. "He is up night and day and frequently up the mast in the crow's nest for there is nearly always an officer up there now scanning the horizon searching for patches of open water," Orde-Lees wrote. As the ship crossed the Antarctic Circle, it became clear that the ice was every bit as bad as the whalers on South Georgia had predicted.

Relaxation and entertainment were critical parts of the schedule Shackleton orchestrated.

Shackleton kept a balance between work and fun, never completely dividing the two yet never letting one overtake the other. Although he planned many special celebrations, he also expected everyone to enjoy their work, which he thought led to greater productivity. It also meant that when the work was done, the men were more likely to spend leisure time together. Shackleton also was expert at balancing his participation in celebrations. He was at the center of everything, yet never became just one of the guys, or singled out any one individual as a particular friend. In later years, Macklin scoffed at attempts by some crewmen to portray themselves as part of an inner circle.

Nothing sums up Shackleton's way of building unity better than the dinner table, where he sought to nourish body and soul. He used meal times to chat and joke with the men, to hear their ideas, to relax as comrades rather than as boss and staff. He frequently ordered up special luxury foods to boost morale and to indulge the men. Some were shocked by the informality. "He associates with us at table without the slightest distinction," Orde-Lees wrote. "In fact, I often think that he errs on the side of over familiarity and does not rebuke members who occasionally address him with a lack of respect that makes my 'service' blood run cold. I think it is that he does not approve of too strict a discipline on an expedition & does not expect it from fellows who have never been subjected to it. In this he is the very reverse of Captain Scott and maybe he is quite right, though I beg to differ on the point myself."

On the *Endurance*'s voyage to Buenos Aires, before Shackleton boarded the ship, mealtimes were haphazard. The officers and professionals ate at four small separate tables. When Shackleton arrived, he arranged to have the whole group of professionals sit together. He sat in the middle of the table, not at the head as the leader of expedition ships typically did. Later, he got out wood and nails and expanded the table to let Orde-Lees join them. Orde-Lees had been eating separately from everyone else, and Shackleton wanted to bring him into the fold.

Shackleton also gathered the crew weekly to listen to the gramophone, play games, perform skits, watch slide shows, sing, and play instruments. "It was a rule to hold a concert on Saturday nights and this rule was very seldom broken," said Wild. Hussey was particularly good on the banjo and Chief Engineer Rickinson sometimes accompanied on the fiddle. More important, Saturday was the night the crew indulged in a time-honored custom at sea, a drink to loved ones: "To our sweethearts and wives, may they never meet!" Shackleton allowed alcohol at celebrations, but only enough to create a relaxed atmosphere, not enough to allow anyone to get drunk.

The Boss joined in simple pastimes: a word game or puzzle, a game of bridge or a lively debate. He insisted that everyone participate, to avoid having the men break up into cliques. Isolation and homesickness could destroy the morale of a crew.

When the ship first got stuck the men started playing a "game of elimination," in which one man leaves the room and comes back in, and with questions that could only be answered yes or no, figures out what has been hidden. For a while, there was a craze for mock trials.

Another time, a singing contest was held after which the men unanimously, and wisely, awarded the prize to the Boss. "His voice is quaint, vacillating between sharps and flats in a most unique manner," Hurley wrote. Capt. Worsley echoed a common refrain: "He is the life and soul of half the skylarking and fooling in the ship."

One day in May, all the men shaved their heads. It was "a form of mid-winter madness," Hurley wrote. Everyone sat to have his head shaved. "It caused much amusement, and luxuriant curls, bald pates and parted crowns soon became akin. . . . We resemble a cargo of convicts."

At first there were some on the *Endurance* who complained about all the diversions. Orde-Lees, of course, was one. "I hate them," he complained. "One is made to sing and I really sing rottenly. Then one is stunk out with tobacco smoke let alone alcoholic fumes. I suppose it's all right for those who smoke and appreciate the liquor but for those who don't it is a nauseating penance. There is no doubt though that teetotalism and conviviality are somewhat incompatible and it is probably this that has mitigated more than any other factor against the abstainee's propaganda."

By the end of the *Endurance* ordeal a year and a half later, however, Orde-Lees would be so caught up in one celebration that he would call it one of the happiest days of his life, despite the fact that the men had fallen into desperate straits.

Shackleton faithfully kept up traditions and holiday rituals. For Christmas 1914 on the *Endurance,* the wardroom was decorated for dinner and small gifts were put at everyone's plate. Some of the men had saved gifts from home to be opened on the holiday. They enjoyed a feast of turtle soup, whitebait, jugged hare, Christmas pudding, mince pies, dates, figs, and crystallized fruits. Drinks of rum and stout were passed around. In the evening, the men joined in a sing-along.

On Christmas Day 1901, Shackleton was marching on the "Great Southern Journey" to the Pole with Robert Scott and Edward Wilson. They had been looking forward to their special yuletide meal. Scott had promised double portions of their otherwise skimpy provisions. As the men were settling down to dinner, Shackleton pulled a spare sock out of his bundle and digging deep into the toe produced, as Scott called it, "a noble plum pudding." He dug around in his bag and presented a piece of artificial holly to use as decoration. As hungry and weakened as Shackleton was, he had saved this for the holiday surprise.

The *Endurance* crew even celebrated Christmas 1915, which

they spent stranded on an ice floe without a ship. Even so, the men were indulged with what few delicacies remained: anchovies in oil, baked beans, "and jugged hare made a glorious mixture such as we have not dreamed of since our school days," Shackleton wrote in *South*.

Shackleton's efforts to unite his crew were rewarded when the situation got worrisome. There was no summer that year in the Weddell Sea, Wild complained. On January 18, 1915, the *Endurance* was "frozen in" just one day's sail from the designated landing spot. "We could see the land we were making for about forty miles away but so far as effecting a landing was concerned it might as well have been four thousand," Wild wrote in his memoirs.

The men didn't blame Shackleton at all for getting them into this predicament. If anything, they felt sorry that he was the one person among them who faced personal disaster, losing his money, his patrons' trust, and perhaps his hard-earned reputation. "Old Cautious" Shackleton was beginning to worry about the safety of the ship. But Shackleton the optimist wasn't giving up yet. Other expeditions had been forced to winter in the frozen seas. All that was needed was a sturdy ship and calm waters under the ice. Every so often, the crew's hopes were lifted by the sight of a large "lead," or new channel of water, as the pack ice cracked and separated. All hands rushed to the deck. Then no sooner would the ship inch forward than it would become surrounded again. Eventually, the leads became rare and it became clear that they were stuck for good.

As far as the eye could see, a thick crust of ice covered the Weddell Sea. Wild remembered walking with Shackleton and Worsley on the ice near the ship and seeing a huge, flat floe. Worsley stopped and said, "Oh boys, what a jolly fine football ground this will make." Shackleton replied, "Well Wuzzles, I have about given up hope of getting out this year but you needn't rub it in so cheerfully."

Soon the men were playing hockey, soccer, moonlight soccer,

chess, cards, dominoes, and myriad other games on the ice and on the ship. "We seem to be a wonderfully happy family but I think Sir Ernest is the real secret of our unanimity," wrote Orde-Lees. "Considering our divergent aims and our differences of station it is surprising how few differences of opinion occur."

The men even made a game of trying to get the ship out of the ice. Worsley described an attempt to "sally" the ship, whereby the crew ran from side to side on the ship's deck trying to rock it free. The deck was so crowded with dog kennels and supplies the men had to squeeze through a tight aisle. "Each falls over the other amidst much laughter and merriment but without much effect on the ship. We next jump simultaneously with the order, 'One, two, three, jump.' Still she remained inert and we pick up the double, all hands stamping hard to double time. This had the desired effect. . . . This mode of salubrious exercise and merriment puts the ship in a position to take advantage of the first opening."

Whatever was ahead, the men were behind their leader, prepared to brave the ordeal together. "We are now six months out from England and during the whole of this time we have all pulled well together and with an almost complete lack of friction," Capt. Worsley wrote just after the ship became stuck. "A more agreeable set of gentlemen and good fellows one could not wish for shipmates."

SHACKLETON'S WAY
OF FORGING A UNITED AND LOYAL TEAM

- Take the time to observe before acting, especially if you are new to the scene. All changes should be aimed at improvements. Don't make changes just for the sake of leaving your mark.

- Always keep the door open to your staff members, and be generous with information that affects them. Well-informed employees are more eager and better prepared to participate.

- Establish order and routine on the job so all workers know where they stand and what is expected of them. The discipline makes the staff feel they're in capable hands.

- Break down traditional hierarchies and cliques by training workers to do a number of jobs, from the menial to the challenging.

- Where possible, have employees work together on certain tasks. It builds trust and respect and even friendship.

- Be fair and impartial in meting out compensations, workloads, and punishments. Imbalances make everyone feel uncomfortable, even the favored.

- Lead by example. Chip in sometimes to help with the work you're having others do. It gives you the opportunity to set a high standard and shows your respect for the job.

- Have regular gatherings to build esprit de corps. These could be informal lunches that allow workers to speak freely outside the office. Or they could be special holiday or anniversary celebrations that let employees relate to each other as people rather than only as colleagues.

WORKING IT IN

Eric Miller, senior adviser for investment bank Donaldson, Lufkin & Jenrette, is impressed by how adroitly Shackleton knit the individual personalities of his crew into one cohesive unit. "He had some weak members, but he blended them in so they were neutralized," he says. "He never showed them his personal disappointments or ever stooped to vindictiveness."

Mr. Miller, who writes commentaries for DLJ's *Portfolio Manager,* a weekly newsletter from San Francisco, recounted the saga of the *Endurance* in his column of August 25, 1999. Shackleton "inspired unshakable confidence in his decisions and won the tenacious loyalty of his men," wrote Mr. Miller, who has been a keen observer and analyst of business trends for more than three decades. He discovered Shackleton after a client gave him Alfred Lansing's *Endurance* to read. The resulting column "hit a nerve" with his readers, he says, and was one of his most popular. He sees the reaction as evidence of people's constant craving for heroes— a craving that has intensified in recent years as peace and prosperity have left us without great challenges, which are the traditional sources of spectacular leadership.

For Mr. Miller, the *Endurance* tale is "a wonderful example and exhilarating story of the human capabilities" to overcome adversity. As a former marine officer in Korea, Mr. Miller admires Shackleton's concern for the safety of all his men. He is particularly struck by how well Shackleton was able to personalize his communication with his officers and men.

Shackleton was far ahead of his time, Mr. Miller says—more democratic than his peers, and more responsive to individual needs. His methods and ideas about the structure of work are only now coming into wide acceptance, he adds, as "organizations have become more horizontal and less hierarchical."

More open organizations have become possible, he believes, as the economy has come to be driven by the technology and service sectors and has moved away from traditional heavy manufacturing. He notes, in particular, the way leaders at Intel and other Silicon Valley companies were pioneers in abolishing the symbols and perks of stratified organizations, such as closed-door offices and privileged parking spaces near the front door for executives only. Now, he adds, it's commonplace for even CEOs to be on a first-name basis with employees at all levels.

Mr. Miller also admires Shackleton's gift for mixing labor and diversion. Shackleton knew when "to encourage a little celebration and enjoyment of something that the men would consider a delicacy," he says, noting that the men look surprisingly well in photographs taken during the *Endurance* expedition. "He was able to join in and participate in both fun and labor without the sacrifice of authority and respect," Mr. Miller wrote. "Everyone participated in the chores, including the scientific experts, and his own physical strength and fortitude proved inspiring."

In today's progressive companies, he says, the formal office party has been replaced by company outings, softball games, and spontaneous celebrations on a smaller scale—of birthdays, a job well done, a good workplace idea, or a sports-team victory.

Mr. Miller has kept his eye on management trends during his forty-five-year career, almost half of which has been spent at DLJ—mostly in its New York headquarters. For twenty years, he has been a host at seminars for top institutional clients on business issues such as leadership, management, and strategic planning.

He has witnessed enormous change in the workplace over the course of his career, few more significant than the empowerment of individuals within the corporation. The gradual blurring of rigid lines of command, with managers and their subordinates working on a more equal footing, "encourages self-reliance and resiliency," he says. Today, employees are expected to exercise initiative; they seldom wait passively for marching orders from headquarters. There simply isn't time for old-style, hierarchical patterns of decision making. "The pace of technological change and global competition demands a faster response time and quicker adaptation," he says.

The diversity of the U.S. workforce—which grew out of the civil rights and women's movements and began to have an impact on corporations in the 1970s—has been the most profound change he has seen in the workplace. Even the "white shoe" investment business, long a conservative bastion of all-male privilege, now reflects the changing demographic realities. The recognition among America's corporate leadership that "nobody has a monopoly on ideas" is a healthy development, he says. Creative solutions come from tapping a more varied pool of talent and from a lively exchange of ideas.

American companies have embraced flexibility and diversity at a much faster pace than their competition in other industrial nations, Mr. Miller observes. This, he suggests, has helped stoke the enormous economic boom that began in the 1990s. The transformation all sounds decidedly Shackletonian, as Mr. Miller defines its essence: "Spirit, energy, and change."

4

GETTING THE BEST FROM
EACH INDIVIDUAL

He led, he did not drive.

—G. Vibert Douglas, geologist, *Quest*

Scott Polar Research Institute

PITCHING IN

Frank Wild, under Shackleton's tutelage, went from a seaman to a skilled second in command able to take the Boss's place in his absence. Shackleton took an interest in the professional and personal development of every man on his crew. As part of his effort to make all of them well-rounded seamen, he made sure everyone kept meeting new challenges.

THE *ENDURANCE* WAS STUCK. THE CREW TRIED FOR WEEKS to break out of the pack ice toward channels of water, but it was no use. On February 24, Shackleton ceased all regular routine on the ship—rendering it, in effect, a winter station. "We could see our base, maddening, tantalizing," Dr. Macklin said. "Shackleton at this time showed one of his sparks of real greatness. He did not rage at all, or show outwardly the slightest sign of disappointment; he told us simply and calmly that we must winter in the pack, explained its dangers and possibilities; never lost his optimism, and prepared for winter."

The best the men could hope for now was that the ship would withstand the polar winter and be freed in the spring thaw, some nine months away. Shackleton, in his way, would manage to expand that shred of hope to sustain his men until then.

For now, the ship's officers and seamen found themselves without a job. All that training to make each crew member a good sailor was for naught. Shackleton needed to find a way to tackle the crew's crushing disappointment, boredom, and fears. He worked to maintain the established routine and structure so that the crew felt secure. He then focused on making sure every man had the strength to pull through the ordeal ahead. They trusted that their leader would take care of everything. And he did. Shackleton shouldered the entire burden of the dilemma leaving his men free to focus on the work at hand.

Shackleton gave all his men equal attention, kindly nurturing back to health one of his least favorite crewmen with the same close attention he gave one of his fondest friends who fell ill. No one had to earn his respect and attention—he gave it freely.

Ultimately, Shackleton won the crew's unwavering loyalty with his extraordinary ability to communicate and connect personally. His contact with his men was constant, friendly, instructive, and often fun. "He led mentally and physically and gave a sense to the individual that he, the individual, was a most important part of the whole show," wrote G. Vibert Douglas, *Quest* geologist. "I'd say Shackleton was very generous in his acknowledgement of his men. There was a warmth about him."

The crewmen's diaries show a surprising lack of concern about being trapped in the ice. Instead, they wrote about the weather, books they were reading from the ship's extensive library, outings, and the trivialities of daily living. They were almost self-conscious about how happy they were. They knew all the horror stories about polar exploration and considered themselves relatively fortunate.

Again, Shackleton set the tone by his own example. "His unfailing cheeriness means a lot to a band of disappointed explorers like ourselves," Orde-Lees wrote. "He is one of the greatest optimists I have ever known. He is not content with saying, 'It will all come right in the end.' It is always otherwise with him. He merely says that this is but a little setback not altogether unforeseen and he immediately commences to modify his program to accord with it, even working his future plans out to given dates and to meet various possible contingencies."

Shackleton kept the atmosphere light through various antics. Early on, he unveiled the experimental motor vehicle, to the delight of the men and the excitement of the dogs. "Marston takes charge of the machine and in inimitable style dispenses imaginary ice creams to the crowd & bystanders, some of whom give very credible representations of small cockney boys," wrote Capt. Worsley. Hurley filmed the event.

Shackleton believed in the importance of
creature comforts in maintaining morale and let
each man put his personal stamp on his surroundings.

The Boss never insisted on uniformity. He preferred creative thinkers to workers who were merely competent. During the *Nimrod* expedition, Shackleton had made a game out of the building, decorating, and naming of private sleeping quarters inside the winter hut. He wrote in his book, *The Heart of the Antarctic,* that building living quarters "is not so trivial a matter as may appear to some readers, for during the winter months the inside of the hut was the whole inhabited world to us." He wrote that one cubicle was so neat and elegant as to be dubbed "No. 1 Park Lane." In another one, the artist Marston had created the illusion of a cozy home by painting a fire burning in a fireplace with a vase of flowers on the mantel. One of the inhabitants of the "Rogues' Retreat" was so excited about constructing his bed that the work proceeded with the utmost secrecy in the storage room. But he forgot to account for the doorway and had to saw the bed in half to get it out. To this day, visitors to the explorers' huts comment on the coziness of the Shackleton quarters.

On the *Endurance,* Shackleton decided that the quarters occupied by the officers and scientists were too cold for the coming winter months. In March, he ordered all hands to help move deeper into the ship where it was warmer. He let the men choose their roommates. The upper deck was cleared of the dog kennels—which were moved to the ice—and the supplies and gear were put in their place. The hold was converted into a living and dining area with cubicles lining the sides. Between the two rows of cubicles a table was set up. The men facetiously called the new room "The Ritz." All meals were taken there instead of the wardroom, and they were prompt: breakfast at 9 A.M., lunch at 1 P.M., tea at 4 P.M., and dinner at 6 P.M.

The former wardroom became living quarters for the more senior men: Wild, Worsley, Crean, and Marston. They dubbed it "The Stables." Other cubicles were given names that reflected their occupants' personalities, such as "The Anchorage" for the ship's two officers, "Auld Reekie" for the Scottish scientists, and "The Knuts," a play on the "nuts" and bolts of the engineers' trade. When anyone had spare time, he worked on his room. Hurley wrote that Marston had created "a sort of opium den settee about 4 by 4.5 feet, which really occupies almost the entire available space of the cubicle."

By March 10, everyone moved into the new quarters. Only the Boss stayed put in the captain's cabin, far from everyone else.

Shackleton insisted on healthy diet, exercise,
and reasonable safety measures, believing
physical and mental acumen were closely linked.

Shackleton provided what was needed to make each person physically and mentally fit to meet the challenges of his job. He himself seemed to maintain a positive frame of mind and a hardy, powerful physique without much effort. As for the others, he encouraged them to combine healthful eating habits with rigorous sport and some means of relaxation. He allowed them a great deal of time outside the ship on the pack ice. He was also emphatic about no one's risking injury in unnecessary horseplay.

At this point in the expedition, the crew members were pleasantly surprised by their good health—though that was partly the benefit of living in a germ-free environment.

In March, with winter coming, the truly frigid temperatures began creeping in. It became more difficult to move about the ship. The surface of the pack ice was marked by large ridges of ice formed by the crashing floes. The only smooth areas were atop the new ice that formed on open leads. (One man noted that four-week-old ice was 13.5 inches thick.) One such area, about 50 yards wide, was 250 yards from the ship. A mile away on the other side was a similar surface. The men beat a well-marked path to both. They looked for areas where new ice formed salty tufts, called "ice flowers." This rough terrain provided a good grip for their boots. "On these fields we spent many a happy hour," Macklin said. "All hands used to turn out and showed the greatest keenness; we were all in the pink of condition; the keen air gave an additional fillip, and the amount of energy expended was prodigious."

The men played soccer and hockey, raced the dogs, and took long walks. Orde-Lees even rode his cherished bicycle that he brought along on the expedition. Once he ventured too far and lost his way in the winter night. Shackleton forbade him to use the bicycle again, a decision that hurt Orde-Lees deeply. But the Boss was adamant about no unnecessary injuries. When Able Seaman McLeod once got lost, he begged his rescuers not to tell Shackleton, knowing full well it would mean an end to the long, solitary walks he was fond of taking. In another incident, the men were playing hockey when Seaman McCarthy was hit in the face and had to have his lip stitched. Worsley wrote that it happened "not to be seen by Sir E., who invariably raises hell if anyone gets injured in any way unnecessarily."

In an attempt to prevent anyone from getting lost in the dark on the ice as the long winter began to set in, Shackleton had the sailors create a circle of ice mounds around the ship and string wire between them so they could feel their ways back even in a blizzard. Photographer Frank Hurley, also an experienced electrician, fixed lights around the ship on poles twenty feet tall to light the floe. The Boss even held emergency drills. If there was any major break in the pack ice, the men were to get themselves and the dogs on board quickly.

The *Endurance* carried a good supply of food, but the men had to eat fresh meat to prevent scurvy. The seamen fought Shackleton at first. They didn't want to eat food from the sea when there were expensive canned goods to enjoy. The Boss had to use psychology. According to geologist James Wordie, when the first seal of the expedition was shot by Wild in December, the Boss went to the deck to admire the kill and announced that there was only enough meat for the wardroom, where the officers and professionals dined. "The mess-deck will have to wait for the next one," he said. Shortly after, the seamen dispatched a representative to demand on their behalf their contracted 25 percent of all provisions. The Boss gave it to them, and they never rejected their portions of seal and penguin again.

There was no leader to take care of such details of diet and safety on the other side of the continent, where the Ross Sea party of the expedition was laying food depots for the planned crossing. In contrast to the good health and safety record enjoyed by the *Endurance* men—and the *Nimrod* crew before them—the Ross Sea party lost three men unnecessarily. One refused to eat the fresh seal and penguin meat needed to build up a reserve of vitamin C for the long trek ahead, complaining he didn't like the taste. During the journey inland, he succumbed to scurvy and died. Two other men, who were also suffering from scurvy, were killed when they ignored the pleas of their companions and tried to cross over water that didn't have a solid frozen crust. They vanished and were never heard from again.

Shackleton made sure each man
had challenging and meaningful work.

With all the ship's main work halted, Shackleton had to find everyone tasks that were deemed important to the expedition or the crew. Most of the effort was aimed at improving living conditions for the men and their animals, continuing the scientific projects, and practicing for the Antarctic crossing, which the men still hoped was only delayed.

The scientists and artists were occupied exploring and recording their fascinating new surroundings, using some relatively new inventions. Physicist Reginald James and Navigating Officer Hubert Hudson got some of the officers and seamen to help them rig a wireless receiver in an unsuccessful attempt to receive a transmission from the Falkland Islands. James also observed the stars and did other scientific work, such as studying atmospheric, ice, and water conditions, and magnetic variations. James Wordie, the geologist, and Robert Clark, the biologist, drilled holes in the ice to sound depths and took samples of mud. Capt. Frank Worsley impressed colleagues by making a tide gauge for estimating the rate of the ice drift. Leonard Hussey took meteorological readings.

Hurley helped Hussey take wind readings, and was generally of service to everyone. He busily started developing the film footage he had shot, setting up a makeshift darkroom and hanging the film to dry in a refrigerator. He took and developed more pictures of the men, the ship, the dogs, and the ice. He also gave occasional weekend lectures, showing slides of New Zealand, Australia, and Borneo. The men's favorite featured native women. Hurley even devised a thaw box for the seal meat used for dog food. Instead of hacking at a block frozen solid, the meat was put in the box attached to the stove and within a day could be cut with a knife.

George Martson painted and sometimes mended boots. Second Officer Thomas Crean took charge of sledges and sledging gear. Third Officer Alfred Cheetham continued to be responsible for the seamen. The men erected a hut for science readings and a shelter for cutting up the seals killed in the hunt. The seamen went out with a large sledge to get fresh ice every day, to be melted on board for water. One of the advantages of polar exploration is that water is abundant and doesn't have to be carried. When salt water freezes, the salt leaches out.

Far from getting bored, the men felt busy. "I am sure that plenty of hard work is a fine thing down here," Orde-Lees wrote. "At present I never seem to have time to do half the things I want to do and my only fear is that I may one day get ahead of my tasks and find myself in the unenviable position of having nothing to do but read, sleep and eat."

Shackleton had already decided back in South Georgia who would go with him on the continental crossing, though he didn't broadcast his choices: Wild, Crean, Macklin, Hurley, and Marston. All but Macklin were experienced in the Antarctic. Each was given a team of nine dogs to prepare for the crossing, with a sixth, Dr. McIlroy, taking the team the Boss would use. These "dog wallahs," as the men caring for the teams were known, were expected to train, feed, tend, and exercise the dogs, finding in each pack a lead dog around which to organize a team. As a tribute to the Boss, the men had given many of the dogs names that began with an *s*, such as Saint, Sailor, Shakespeare, and Sampson.

When it was decided that the noisy animals took up too much room on the ship, all hands were put to work building "dogloos" and even a "pigloo" for the remaining pig. The men got carried away building elaborate "crystal" doghouses fashioned from blocks of ice and snow and sealed by pouring water over them. One had the tapered spires of a church and another the elaborate porticos of a mansion. Unfortunately "Dog Town" didn't survive the breaking and crashing ice floes for long.

By April, only fifty-four of the expedition's sixty-nine dogs had survived. Some were sick with worms as the worm powder had been inadvertently left behind in England. The effort of nursing the dogs back to health shows how Shackleton built a balanced work environment around a simple task. He first made clear the significance of the work to the expedition: The dogs had to be strong and well trained for the crossing. He then gave bottom-line responsibility to the men in charge. Finally, he made the task a source of pride by encouraging competition, which resulted in an elaborate Antarctic Dog Derby.

It all began on one June day with Hurley boasting over lunch that his team was the fastest, and Sir Ernest egged him on. Bets were booked. Capt. Worsley waged his week's chocolate against

Wordie's that Wild's team would win. "This starts the ball rolling and it is arranged that all teams compete the next day in a timed race," Worsley wrote. "It was under half a mile." Wild's team, the favorite, beat Hurley's. In a rematch, Wild's team won again but was disqualified when Shackleton fell off the sledge just ten yards from the finish line. "He was most disgusted with himself and insisted on paying off all bets," the captain wrote.

Shackleton matched personality types with work responsibilities.

Even while he was training all the men to do all the ship's work, the Boss was observing everyone's personality. He wanted to put each person in a long-term job he enjoyed and for which he was best suited. He watched as each took care of the dogs on a rotating basis, then selected dog-team leaders. Shackleton figured the best work came from those with a particular interest in the job, and the dogs benefited from the dedicated care of one owner.

As another example, Orde-Lees, hired as a motor expert, was a pack rat and obsessed about the possibility of running short of supplies. The crew members knew that if anything was missing on the ship, it would likely be under Orde-Lee's pillow or bed. So Shackleton made this hoarder the storekeeper. To some it seemed like putting the fox in charge of the henhouse, but Shackleton knew this job would allay Orde-Lee's anxieties and prevent the possibility of having to deal with other problems down the road. Orde-Lees was delighted: "It is most awfully fortunate for me that Sir Ernest should have put me on to this work which is so especially congenial to me."

Shackleton gave his men constant feedback, praising their efforts and correcting their mistakes.

Shackleton was dedicated to making each person under him a solid sailor. He believed in hands-on training—but only when it was needed. He expected the men to do well and intervened only when they did not. He "has never once come 'spying' in my store-rooms nor even asked me to render an account of my steward-ship," Orde-Lees explained. By conveying such trust, Shackleton got the best work from each man. As evidence of Shackleton's light touch, the confident and competent Hurley rarely mentioned Shackleton in his diary until he began sharing a tent with him months later.

As the situation for the men of the *Endurance* grew more dire, however, Shackleton became less willing to delegate responsibility. In July, for example, one distant storm caused the ice floes to move rapidly and collide. McNeish noted that he was ordered to report conditions to Shackleton every half hour. In every situation Shackleton was there with an encouraging word. Appointed interim cook, Orde-Lees knew that whenever he botched meals in the kitchen he always had one customer. "I unfortunately forgot some jam tarts in the oven today and they got burnt as black as a hat," he wrote. "Sir Ernest good-naturedly attempted to eat one but it was too far gone, even for him."

Shackleton was patient and generous with his time, and the men were flattered by the extra attention. On Shackleton's *Quest* expedition, the *Quest,* one of his men, the Boy Scout James Marr, explained his appreciation of his boss's tutelage. Marr had unlashed a drum stored on the ship's deck and was opening it when Shackleton gave "a needed lesson in common-sense *sailorizing.*"

"Don't try to do too many things on your own until you've got the hang of them," Shackleton told him. "If any accident happened and that drum fetched away, the boatswain would be blamed, because safe storage is his job. When you mix in with another man's job, always remember that he might have to take blame that's rightly due to you." Marr watched the Boss lash up the drum while explaining: "You've put on a slippery hitch. Here's the right way, and it's the right way that counts at sea."

"With all the weight of responsibility he carried on his shoulders, and all his worries—for he had many—he still found time to interest himself in an obscure Scout," Marr wrote. "But he was like that; I think that was one of the qualities that made him great."

Shackleton related to every person under
him as a human being, not only as a worker.

The Boss developed a personal relationship with each crew member. He wanted his men to like and respect him as well as honor his position. His conversations never seemed contrived or staged to the men. Just as Shackleton always preferred face-to-face meetings with his backers, he liked to deal with his men one-on-one. No praise or condemnation was ever done through a middleman or in a circuitous way. Shackleton spoke with the highest and the lowest on his crew, finding some common ground on which to meet.

He was particularly solicitous of his men after they were frozen in and as the polar winter was drawing near—the sun set in May for four months. Most were experiencing the grim darkness for the first time, and Shackleton took pains to put them in the proper frame of mind to get through it.

Dr. Macklin, then twenty-four years old, said that when Shackleton came across a crewman walking alone, "he would get into conversation and talk to you in an intimate sort of way, asking you little things about yourself—how you were getting on, how you liked it, what particular side of the work you were enjoying most— all that sort of thing. . . . This communicativeness in Shackleton was one of the things his men valued in him; it was also, of course, a most effective way of establishing good relations with a very mixed company."

Shackleton liked to chat with his men in the quiet early morning hours when there was a particularly relaxed atmosphere. Raymond Priestley wrote about him aboard the *Nimrod:* "When everyone else had retired to bed, the night watchman was never surprised when Shackleton joined him for a half-hour's chat or to smoke a cigarette in the small hours before himself turning in."

The older the Boss got the more he listened. As a young man, he did more lecturing. Explorer Louis Bernacchi recalled the time on the *Discovery* when Shackleton came to relieve him of night watch at 4 A.M. "full of verses and warmth-giving navy cocoa. I lacked enthusiasm. Shackleton was a poet and that morning poetically very wide awake, and in his wheedling Irish manner he kept me from my waiting bunk reciting endless verses in the voice and manner of an old-time tragedian."

Books were always a refuge and a tool for Shackleton. On, the *Endurance,* Shackleton kept the ship's library in his cabin. That way he could always run into his crewmen and have something to talk about. William Bakewell said Shackleton "would ask me many questions and my opinion of each book." Even back on the *Discovery,* when the relationship between Scott and Shackleton began to deteriorate on the Southern Journey, the two men kept the lines of communication open by reading poetry aloud in the evenings.

Shackleton held small celebrations that recognized the individual.

The Boss balanced the group festivities with those honoring one person. The celebrations at Christmas and other holidays were held with great fanfare and respect for tradition. But Shackleton also relied on celebrations and games in which individuals could demonstrate their talents, personalities, and optimism.

The most popular of these small fetes were birthdays. They weren't routine or empty gestures but rather clever, personalized affairs, usually involving a toast at the end of the evening. They were popular with the crew. On February 14, 1915, the men were out with picks and saws trying to free the ship from the ice. They worked all day in single-digit temperatures chipping ice around the ship into blocks, hauling the huge blocks onto the floe, smashing them and scattering the pieces. All to no avail.

At midnight the men stopped their work, put down their tools, wished Sir Ernest "many happy returns of the day," and gave him three cheers. The Boss was forty-one years old.

On April 18, Hurley reported that Wild's birthday was celebrated with a drink, music, and "an excellent cake of wondrous rainbow colors" made by the cook. The next day Stephenson's birthday was celebrated with a bottle of rum. Orde-Lees marked his birthday on May 23. "This day I celebrated my birthday believing myself to be thirty-six. I don't feel it, but my friends say I look it every day," he said. On September 1, Macklin's birthday was celebrated by giving him the place of honor, front and center, in a group photo. On the eleventh of the month, Clark received "numerous letters and cards, stamped and addressed, and a miscellany of generally useless articles. Much merriment is caused by him being compelled to read the contents of his letters at the breakfast table."

Everyone looked forward to June 22, the midwinter's day festival, marking the turning point in the long polar night, after which winter was on the wane. Each man dressed in costume (Shackleton, in top hat, was master of ceremonies) and performed a skit, often skewering their shipmates. Orde-Lees got up at 7 A.M. to decorate the wardroom with flags. The men feasted throughout the day, and in the evening they held an outrageous three-hour show. The seamen were treated to a feast of special foods. They weren't invited to the show, perhaps because Shackleton feared that their seeing the officers cavorting in costumes and being parodied would undermine any position of authority.

Shackleton was tolerant of people's quirks
and foibles. He didn't hesitate to pamper his men.

Shackleton showed remarkable kindness toward his men. When it seemed he couldn't possibly spare the time or energy to make some thoughtful gesture, he did. He was the one person on the ship who forgave Orde-Lees his selfishness and neediness. "He knows one's limitations better than one does oneself and he invariably allows for them," Orde-Lees wrote. "He never expects one to do more than one is capable of."

Orde-Lees had sciatica and suffered a particularly bad bout in late July. Shackleton privately blamed Orde-Lees's carelessness: He had gone out in frigid temperatures "in just the ordinary things one would wear on a mild cold day in England," as Orde-Lees admitted.

Shackleton also suffered recurring bouts of sciatica, so he empathized. Orde-Lees was laid up flat on his back in bed for a week, unable to move from the pain and full of self-pity. Sir Ernest invited him into his cabin. The patient stayed for two weeks, certain he was receiving better care under Shackleton than he could have found in an English hospital. The close quarters must have been extremely uncomfortable. To help his patient's sciatica, the Boss, stoking the small stove, allowed temperatures to climb to sweltering heights night after night.

"Here I have lain in the utmost comfort but severe pain for the last five days while Sir Ernest has coiled himself up as best he could on a narrow little bench much too short for him!" Orde-Lees wrote at the beginning of his stay. "He is a wonderful man. He takes the minimum of sleep; seldom more than three or four hours a night, sometimes less, but how he manages to get even that on such an uncomfortable couch is a puzzle. He looks after me himself with all the tender care of a trained nurse, which indeed he seems to me to be far more than merely my leader and master for the time being. He attends to me himself, making up the fire and making me a cup of tea during the night if I happen to say that I am thirsty, reading to me and always entertaining me with his wonderful conversation, making me forget my pain by joking with me continually just as if I was a spoiled child. What sacrifices would I not make for such a leader as this."

The men, in general, were content. Dr. Macklin noted a conversation that took place one evening when he had taken Alf Cheetham for a ride on his sledge.

"I say, Doctor, don't you think we are better off than the king?" Cheetham asked.

"I don't know, Cheetham," Macklin replied.

"Well, I'm happy, Doctor, and you're happy, and here we are sitting on a sledge driving smoothly home and looking at the wonders of the world; it goes into your soul, like, don't it, Doctor? The king with all his might and with all his power couldn't come here and enjoy what I'm enjoying."

But the crew's peaceful world was about to be shattered as the ice started to move violently. As early as July 31, Shackleton was quietly preparing for various possible scenarios. He asked Orde-Lees to make a list of food supplies needed to sustain twenty-eight men for seventy-two days and put those stores on deck in case they had to quickly abandon ship. Orde-Lees seemed privy to Shackleton's long-range plans: "We might be able to sledge over the ice to either Paulet Island where there is known to be a large [food] depot, or even to Wilhelmina Bay where there is believed to be a whaling station," he wrote. "It would be a big undertaking, but no doubt under Sir Ernest we should do it, living on seal & penguin until rescued."

At this point, Orde-Lees noted that Shackleton was getting very little sleep, and arranged to move out of his cabin. It was the first hint of the trouble that was coming later on. Shackleton was up the entire night of August 7, the eve of the anniversary of the *Endurance's* departure for the open sea. The men had witnessed a crash of two huge floes that sent up a ridge of ice some twenty feet high. The crystal dog kennels were crushed into powder. Storms were kicking up. The men were frightened. From his sickbed, Orde-Lees wrote that he was reminded of an earthquake he had experienced as a child. He was surprised by the eerie silence during an emergency drill, as all hands brought the dogs on board. "There is no confusion, no shouting, no noise except the barking of the bewildered dogs & the soft patter of the fur shod feet of the men as each dog is rapidly removed from his kennel on the floe & brought to his appointed place on board." The work, he said, was carried out with great smoothness and precision.

Two ice floes six feet thick held the ship in a vice-like grip, cracking the beams. Each crew member, as part of the emergency plan, took an hour's watch for an around-the-clock alert. The temperature was at zero. But as suddenly as it started the ice let up and relaxed its grip.

The crew endured similar episodes for two more agonizing months. But the men didn't give way to despair. The polar spring was approaching and it seemed for a time that they had survived the ordeal and could soon limp toward land. Orde-Lees wrote on October 11, 1915, that "everything on board [was] dripping wet with thaw." The men began to think about moving back to the upper deck and heading toward civilization. "One longs to see some rocks even, let alone grass, trees & animals," Orde-Lees wrote. "Still, we have nothing to grumble about as it is, for we have warmth & comfort and the very best of food, & moreover this exhilarating climate makes one feel always fit & well."

Just days before the final attack by the ice began, R. W. James objected to being awakened in the middle of the night to stand watch. Several others grumbled when Shackleton ordered that the boilers be fired up in anticipation of the need for steam power. On October 24, the ship was again attacked by the moving ice. All hands went onto the floes with picks and shovels to cut trenches in a vain attempt to relieve the pressure. The ship began to take on water. The men started up the pumps. But even with the pumps working day and night, and McNeish building a small dam, the men couldn't stay ahead of the water. The men began to remove the stores, all the while nervous about the loud noise of rushing water and cracking beams.

On October 27, the weather cleared and temperatures dipped to −15 degrees Fahrenheit. Hurley heard a deafening alarm made by the groaning planks, the crunching of the ice, and the wailing dogs. He wrapped his photo album in waterproof cloth. On the deck, the crew was stacking up stores. At 7 P.M., the order was given to lower the three lifeboats. It was no use. The men had to abandon ship. In the midst of the ensuing chaos, Shackleton observed the situation, holding on to the rigging and smoking a cigarette "with a serious but somewhat unconcerned air," Orde-Lees recalled. Even then, Shackleton offered personal comments as his men filed past. "To each of us, as occasion offered, he said a word or two of encouragement, such as 'Don't forget to take such and such a thing with you if we have to leave the ship.' To me, 'Mind you put your old diary in my bag as it has been kept rather more regularly than mine, I believe.'"

Shackleton followed the men onto the ice. They would make scavenging trips to the ship for another month, but she was no longer home or safe haven. Orde-Lees wrote: "Sir Ernest is now confronted with as big a problem as he has, I suppose, ever tackled: how to extricate us from this serious dilemma and ensure reaching civilization with the whole party alive & well."

SHACKLETON'S WAY
OF DEVELOPING INDIVIDUAL TALENT

- Create a work environment comfortable enough to entice professionals to spend the greater part of their waking hours there. Allow for some personal preferences.

- Be generous with programs that promote the well-being of your staff. Healthy bodies and minds are more productive.

- Make sure each employee has challenging and important work. Even the lowest-ranking workers must feel they are making a valuable and appreciated contribution to the company.

- Match the person to the position. Be observant of the types of people who are working for you and what jobs might best suit their personalities as well as their experience.

- Give consistent feedback on performance. Most workers feel they don't get nearly enough words of praise and encouragement.

- Strive for work relationships that have a human as well as professional element. No matter how large your company, get to know as many employees as possible. Memorize their interests so you can chat about something other than work.

- Reward the individual as well as the group. Public acknowledgment of a job well done—a birthday or a work anniversary—will make an employee feel appreciated.

- Be tolerant. Know each employee's strengths and weaknesses, and set reasonable expectations. Occasionally indulging individuals, even if you think they're being too needy, can have a powerful effect, especially in high-stress situations.

WORKING IT IN

Luke O'Neill was looking for a name for an innovative high school he dreamed of opening in Massachusetts for students who felt frustrated by traditional education. He wanted the school to inspire young people to forget any past failures and to focus on their strengths so they could succeed in ways they never thought possible. The name had to convey this commitment to individual achievement.

Mr. O'Neill still hadn't found a name by the time he graduated in 1995 from Harvard Business School, where he had gone to learn the organization and management skills he needed to implement his plan. That summer, a friend handed him Capt. Frank Worsley's book about the *Endurance*. Dazzled by the thrilling story of leadership and survival, he knew he had found the guiding spirit for his school. In 1998, Mr. O'Neill, then thirty-eight years old, opened the doors to Shackleton Schools Inc., with headquarters in Boston and a "base camp" sixty miles away in Ashby.

Today he hopes some day to build a network of half a dozen of the privately funded, nonprofit schools across the country. "Our educational goal is to train students to be leaders, educators, community builders, entrepreneurs, and stewards of the earth," he says.

There are no traditional classrooms for the students—boys and girls ages fourteen to eighteen. The curriculum is based on "learning expeditions" that combine academic disciplines with educational travel. One group, for example, visited towns on both sides of the U.S.–Mexican border to study Spanish language and culture, the environment, and public policy. Students and their instructors spend at least half their time on such expeditions. The rest of the time is spent in internships and working on independent projects in their communities.

It sounds like a school Shackleton would have loved.

"We aim to encounter the world as Shackleton did: to try, to explore and to serve," says Mr. O'Neill. Shackleton's expeditions, he adds, "had more to do with exploring his own potential than exploring the Antarctic."

In that way, two aspects of the school directly parallel Shackleton's story, Mr. O'Neill explains. The first is a real sense of expedition—"to discover what you have, who you are, and what your mission is in life," he says. "The second is a sense of service—to yourself and to the community."

To learn, Mr. O'Neill believes, you have to be put in a situation that triggers emotion. That means taking people out of their routines, either physically or mentally. "You don't learn when you're in your comfort zone, when you're sitting at the same desk every day, in the same place, doing the same thing, and everything is predictable," he says. "The learning zone is where there is a manageable amount of discomfort, and emotions are heightened."

Mr. O'Neill can list example after example of young people he has encountered over the years who have surprised everyone, including themselves, with what they were able to accomplish. One fifteen-year-old student, Bailey Hirss, spent her summer as an intern at Vermont's largest hospital after her first year at Shackleton Schools. She ended up reengineering the hospital's entire internal patient-transport system, organizing paid staff and volunteers. By the end of the summer, the average waiting time for a patient between appointments fell from forty-five minutes to two minutes. The hospital called her the "Volunteer of the Century" and successfully nominated her for the Student Service Award from President Clinton.

Mr. O'Neill showed a Shackleton-like intensity in his bold pursuit of his vision. He says the explorer came to his mind often while trying to raise money and find a suitable place for the school. It had been a long journey to get to that point. It began when Mr. O'Neill was an undergraduate at Georgetown University in Washington, D.C. He had volunteered as a Big Brother and found that working with young people was his calling. He went on to get a degree from

Georgetown Law School, where he worked in the school's Juvenile Justice Clinic, but he was frustrated that as a lawyer he was connecting with young people only after they had gotten into trouble. When he joined a prestigious law firm in Connecticut, he continued to do pro bono legal work in the local juvenile courts and volunteered in the local Boys & Girls Club of Stamford. Eventually, the need to rebuild the club's center led to his decision to work there full time, leaving his corporate-law practice behind. In 1990, his journey led him to a job with Outward Bound, where he raised more than $8.5 million in just four years. He also became an Outward Bound instructor at the Hurricane Island school in Maine. That experience inspired him to open his own schools.

He recalls that during the period before the school acquired its seventy-acre base camp, he felt as though he were living his own *Endurance* experience, isolated and adrift with his crew of students. At that time, the school had to take to the road. Students and instructors slept in tents, used wood stoves, built boats, and generally faced new obstacles every day. "Starting a business is just like a big expedition—you have to be resourceful, resilient, courageous, hardworking, and optimistic," Mr. O'Neill says. "Above all, you must persevere."

Like Shackleton, Mr. O'Neill is fond of the Canadian poet Robert Service and likes to quote this line from *The Call of the Wild:* "The simple things, the true things, the silent men who do things." He says Shackleton was all about doing: He had the courage to pursue a dream and the sense of responsibility to see that it was carried out to its end.

Mr. O'Neill characterized Shackleton's very human approach to his work in an interview with *The Wall Street Journal:* "Never give up, don't be afraid to lead, follow your gut, and remember, it's about people."

5

LEADING EFFECTIVELY
IN A CRISIS

Not only the main problem but its details absorbed him. Food, how to get it, how to eke out our slender stock of preserved food to give the greatest variety to the eternal seal. How to keep everyone employed and cheerful, to keep sleeping bags dry to nip any sign of pessimism in the bud, the best way of keeping the stores ready for an instant shift—all these things and many more occupied his thoughts by day and most of the night.

—Reginald W. James, physicist, *Endurance*

Royal Geographical Society, London

PULLING TOGETHER

Making the stranded crewmen drag the lifeboats over rough, icy terrain was a futile effort and Shackleton knew it, but it provided his men with a sense that they were doing something to get out of their predicament.

THE MEN RUSHED TO SAFETY ON THE ICE, EXHAUSTED FROM their three-day struggle to save the ship. They quickly set up their tents and fell into them. Just as they had dropped off to sleep, a crack in the ice tore through their camp and they had to scramble to another spot for safety. It was suddenly clear they were going to face an extraordinary challenge just to stay alive. The men had expected to be working in relative comfort in a base camp, or to be doing ship's work. Instead, they were stranded on a vast, unstable layer of ice that was their only refuge from the depths of the Weddell Sea or, even worse, the jaws of a killer whale or a sea leopard. And it was –16 degrees Fahrenheit.

Modern readers might think the crew of the *Endurance* was of a different breed—living at a time when men were men and people in general were less pampered. It's true that most of the crew had some experience as sailors or explorers, but several were college-educated professionals in their early twenties and were unprepared for what lay ahead. What's more, as Shackleton once pointed out, "who begs to toil at the ends of the earth but some people of a truly different stripe?"

Consider how Orde-Lees, the storekeeper, regarded his first days on the *Endurance,* a mere fourteen months before he had to abandon ship: "We help ourselves direct from the butter dish and so on in ways too nauseating to mention. It is extraordinary how quickly one relapses into barbarism."

R. W. James, twenty-four, the ship's physicist, was a quiet academic fresh out of school, the butt of ribbing by the others over his fancy scientific instruments. He was reared by two aunts who owned an umbrella shop in London. Except for his extraordinary scientific mind, his background and temperament made him an unusual choice for the job. Alexander Macklin gave him credit for withstanding the whole ordeal, considering he clearly was out of his element. "Seen at base camp doing his own work I am sure he would have appeared a different person and increased considerably in stature," the surgeon said.

Frank Hurley, twenty-nine years old, was intelligent, articulate, talented, and astonishingly resourceful, "a jack of all trades," his colleagues called him. But he was also a feisty maverick and a loner. A friend, Ian Anderson, described him as someone who had a difficult childhood and grew up to be untrusting of others. He used his camera as a shield between himself and the rest of the world, he said. "He had to have a mask," he continued. "Photography was not only a vocation, it was a need."

All the crew had now was each other and the culture and camaraderie that Shackleton had laid as a foundation for their work. It was difficult enough when the ship got stuck and the men had to give up their most important work. Now, they had lost their workplace, their dreams of glory, and even their home. They needed encouragement. Shackleton stepped forward as they were settling into their tents for a second time.

Shackleton addressed his men, leaving no doubt that he was in complete charge and that he would get them through the crisis if they would stick together and trust him to the end.

The Boss gathered the whole group around him and spoke to his men from the heart. He kept his message simple, gave a realistic appraisal of the situation, explained options, and offered a plan of action. He then thanked them for their efforts, and asked them for their support.

As he spoke, he appeared calm, confident, and strong. Years later, several of the men would recall how much his words meant to them at that time. "There was nothing of the nature of a set speech," R. W. James recalled. "He spoke to us in a group, telling us that he intended to march the party across the [ice] to the west . . . that he thought we ought to manage five miles a day, and that if we all worked together it could be done. The necessity seemed obvious. At heart we were probably glad that the time of anxiety as to whether or not we should save the ship was over, and that the job was now up to us. I can't remember the matter being discussed or argued in any way. We were in a mess, and the Boss was the man who could get us out. It is a measure of his leadership that this seemed almost axiomatic."

The men silently swore their loyalty.

"It was a characteristic speech—simple, moving, optimistic and highly effective," Hussey wrote later. "It brought us out of our doldrums, our spirits rose, and we had our supper."

Offering food for comfort was a typical Shackleton way of letting the men talk and relax while the Boss's words sank in. The ordinary routine also showed that everything was going to proceed as normally as possible. After dinner, Shackleton didn't sleep. He paced the floe, looking first at the painful sight of his dying ship, then at the overwhelming scene of his men exposed and vulnerable. Around daybreak at 2 A.M., he called Wild and Hurley to go with him to get some fuel from the ship. After retrieving a couple of cans through great effort, they headed back to camp, leaping across the splitting ice. They transformed two five-gallon watertight tanks pulled from a lifeboat into a stove and quickly prepared piping-hot milk for the men when they awakened. "We three ministering angels went round the tents with the life-giving drink, and were surprised and a trifle chagrined at the matter-of-fact manner in which some of the men accepted this contribution to their comfort. They did not quite understand what work we had done for them in the early dawn," Shackleton wrote in his book *South,* adding, "a little thanks will go a long way on such occasions."

Shackleton was learning what would become very clear to him later: that leaders face an often thankless and lonely job, especially in hard times. His men rarely returned any of the pampering and ego soothing he was so liberally doling out.

**Shackleton flattened what was left
of the hierarchy of authority.**

The men were one body, and Shackleton was the leader. At this point, all titles or social positions were meaningless. "The ship's officers became units with no more authority than the rest of the crowd, and their position on the floe was the same," Macklin said.

The Boss, who asked for no favors himself, insisted on equal treatment for all. Worsley wrote about the night, just after they had abandoned ship, that the extrawarm reindeer sleeping bags were handed out. The bags were in short supply because they had been intended only for the shore party. All twenty-eight men drew lots to see who would be the lucky eighteen. It didn't really matter who won. The Boss made things seem fair and equitable, so no one felt threatened. Those who were stuck with the blanket bags got a reindeer skin to lie on so they wouldn't be less comfortable than the winners, and would feel just as lucky.

Later, in response to complaints that food portions were uneven, Shackleton applied a routine to food distribution that he had devised on the *Discovery* expedition and used on the *Nimrod.* Everyone—including Shackleton—had to take turns getting the food from the cook and bringing it to the tent. There, another man would either close his eyes or turn his back to the food. The carrier would point to a portion and ask him, "Whose?" The man would give a name and that person would get the portion. Everyone had to admit it was fair, even though Macklin wrote that it didn't stop them from looking "a little enviously at the next man's helping, which differs in some especially appreciated detail from one's own."

Looking back at Shackleton from a modern-day perspective, it is clear that he was an astute psychologist. It wasn't as clear then. Macklin noted later that psychology wasn't a very popular subject in Shackleton's time. The Boss was a voracious reader and was likely interested in the theories being put forward by scholars of the time—such as Sigmund Freud and Ivan Pavlov.

In *South,* his own account of the *Endurance* expedition, Shackleton began to mention more and more "the psychological aspect" of his deeds, or "the psychological interest" of his observations.

Shackleton made many contingency
plans in great detail while still remaining flexible.

Shackleton was beginning to put into action many of the ideas and strategies he had meticulously planned on the ship over the previous months. These mainly concerned how to get his men to safety while keeping them united and free of despair. His diary from the months he was stranded on the ship is full of lists and instructions. "The disaster had been looming ahead for many months, and I had studied my plans for all contingencies a hundred times," Shackleton later wrote.

The goal was daunting. The men were more than a thousand miles from any other human beings, and hundreds of miles from terra firma. "The task now was to secure the safety of the party, and to that I must bend my energies and mental power and apply every bit of knowledge that experience of the Antarctic had given me," Shackleton wrote. "The task was likely to be long and strenuous, and an ordered mind and a clear program were essential if we were to come through without loss of life."

When they abandoned ship, they were 500 miles from Wilhelmina Bay on the Antarctic peninsula, where they could hope to be spotted by passing whalers. About 350 miles to the northwest was Paulet Island. The island had a hut on it that Shackleton himself had been hired (by the Argentines some thirteen years before) to have filled with emergency supplies for an expedition. The nearest piece of Antarctic coast was 180 miles away, but it was desolate and was unlikely to be visited by anyone.

The ice floe was drifting clockwise in a northerly direction, bringing them closer to their targets. Meanwhile, the men would march west over land, and when the ice couldn't hold them any longer, they would take to their boats. Twice the Boss attempted marches and twice he called them off. The boats were too heavy to move over the rough terrain, and the precious lifeboats were taking a beating.

Shackleton pared down possessions
to only what was essential for survival.
He was wise about what constituted a necessity.

Shackleton was frugal but not parsimonious. He knew what was important. Happiness and comfort were not expendable. On October 30, the men awoke to an overcast day. They had spent three nights on the ice and Shackleton had decided to start the march toward land. He ordered everyone to carry only two pounds of goods, including six pairs of socks, a spare pair of boots, a pair of fur mittens, and one pound of tobacco or cocoa. Everyone was given his own roll of toilet paper, some of which came to be used as cigarette papers. That left little room for personal gear—typically soap, a brush, toothbrush, and toothpaste. Some took their own spoons. Everything else had to be discarded.

Shackleton set the example, throwing into the snow all his valuable possessions: a gold watch, fifty gold sovereigns, silver brushes and a dressing case, most of the ship's books, and the Bible given by Queen Alexandra—after he tore out the queen's dedication and a verse from Job. Everyone followed suit.

Hussey remembered Shackleton calling him over about that

time to tell him: "I've just been back to the ship. I was in the ward-room—it's in a frightful mess, the beams are snapping like matchsticks, but in the only corner still unharmed I found something of yours. I've dumped it over there with the food stores."

Hussey was surprised to learn it was his banjo. "It's rather heavy. Do you think we ought to take it?" Hussey asked.

"Yes, certainly," was Shackleton's prompt answer. "It's vital mental medicine, and we shall need it."

Their temporary site was called Dump Camp. The men complained, though never to the Boss's face, of the loss of cherished personal items, instruments, polar clothing, and most of all, food. Seaman Tom McLeod rescued the Bible in the belief that discarding it would bring bad luck. At least one other, John Vincent, secretly returned to pick through the riches, and later would pay dearly for his greed. But the Boss couldn't afford to have the men worry about saving things when their own lives were threatened. If Shackleton had any doubts about the need for setting stringent priorities, an encounter with Orde-Lees just after abandoning ship would erase them. Orde-Lees wrote contritely in his diary that he had foolishly asked Shackleton if he had saved his handsome gold cigarette case. "Cigarette case be blowed," Shackleton shot back. "I've just lost a bally ship haven't I?"

When possible, Shackleton helped the men put things behind them, literally and figuratively, by walking away from them. He waited until the last minutes before leaving possessions behind at Dump Camp to order the four puppies and McNeish's cat, Mrs. Chippy, shot. They took too much care. Immediately afterward, he started the march toward land. The dog sledges went first, loaded with supplies, and then the boats, dragged by the men. The lifeboat *Stancomb Wills* was left behind. The boats were extremely heavy and had to be pulled over an icy terrain full of ridges and hummocks. The men made less than three quarters of a mile the first day. The next day they did slightly better: a mile. By the third day, it was clear they were not going to make anywhere near the daily goal Shackleton had set of four to five miles. They would never make it to land in any reasonable time. He halted the march.

It was November 1, 1915; Antarctic spring. The men set up a more comfortable camp, called Ocean Camp, and stayed there until just before Christmas. They used their ingenuity to make it a rough-hewn copy of civilization. Photos of Ocean Camp show laundry drying on a clothesline, a wooden lookout tower, and a large stove. "When the temperature at home is at and below the freezing point and there is a light wind and no sun, one would hardly expect to find people working out in the open, bare-handed, all day and some of them stripped to the waist having a partial bath in the snow water, as many of us were doing here today," wrote Orde-Lees.

The fact that the temperatures were rising into the twenties wasn't as welcome as one might think. The floes softened and occasionally the men fell through a weak spot. Their feet and clothing ranged between damp and soaked. Walking was only slightly better at night when the surface hardened. The men became preoccupied with being constantly wet. The air was too humid to dry their clothes, and there were often snowstorms and rain. The worst thing was at night when their body heat thawed the floor of their tents. "Very warm in the tent, temperature rising to +78!!" Hurley wrote.

Most agonizing was the realization that the ice they were living on was a rather precarious setting. Hurley wrote in his diary on November 7: "It is beyond conception, even to us, that we are dwelling on a colossal ice raft, with but five feet of ice separating us from 2,000 fathoms of ocean and drifting along under the caprices of wind and tides, to heaven knows where!"

Shackleton made sure the men
had a realistic notion of their plight.

Shackleton wanted the men to be happy and confident of survival. He also wanted them to take their situation seriously and assume some of the responsibility for their own fates.

Just after abandoning the ship, Shackleton overheard two of the men ordering tea from the cook. One asked for strong tea, the other for weak. "It was pleasant to know that their minds were untroubled, but I thought the time opportune to mention that the tea would be the same for all hands and that we would be fortunate if two months later we had any tea at all," Shackleton wrote in *South*. "It occurred to me at the time that the incident had psychological interest. Here were men, their home crushed, the camp pitched on the unstable floes, and their chance of reaching safety apparently remote, calmly attending to the details of existence and giving their attention to such trifles as the strength of a brew of tea."

Despite his sympathetic tone, Shackleton was concerned about the men's cavalier attitude toward their circumstances. He immediately cut the food allowance to 9.5 ounces per man per day. That translates to about 1,500 calories, not much for a bunch of cold, wet young men. He only enforced the cutback for a few days, but it drove the point home. The men wrote for years afterward about the hardship they suffered during that time.

The order was reversed after the men had finished salvaging enough provisions from the ship. Hurley captured the mood of the group one day in early November: "The salvage party broke through the deck shortly after 11 A.M. . . . By fishing with boathooks, case after case was directed to the opening from which they emerged buoyantly to the surface. The scene was highly amusing, and reminded me of the juvenile game of fishpond. If one of the fishers brought to light a case of high food value, a great cheer arose. I was just in time to see a keg of soda carbonate greeted with groans. So, in proportion to the relative values of the salvaged cases, so was their appearance greeted with suitable exclamations."

Over time, the men got out three tons of provisions that way. Shackleton calculated that at one pound per day each, the food would last them three months. Everyone got enough to stay healthy, if not sated. "Monotony in the meals, even considering the

circumstances in which we found ourselves, was what I was striving to avoid, so our little stock of luxuries, such as fish paste, tinned
herrings, etc., was carefully husbanded and so distributed as to
last as long as possible," Shackleton wrote.

In fact, the men who had Antarctic experience thought the food
supply was more than adequate. They had been killing seals all
along. Hurley's diary shows him helping the men kill hundreds of
penguins and dozens of seals during the time they lived on the floe.
Hurley described the menu: "Breakfast is fried seal steak, tea, milk
and sugar; lunch is suet pudding & jam, cocoa, milk and sugar;
supper is ham & seal liver hoosh [a combination of stew and hash]
with desiccated potato & flour, cocoa, milk & sugar and digestive
biscuits."

Shackleton kept the malcontents close to him
to contain their effect and to try to win them over.

Shackleton laid the groundwork for the crew's survival on the floe
by his brilliant selection of who would live together in the five
tents, balancing personalities, experience, and attitude in each. He
nipped dissent in the bud, and kept the naysayers close by.

In his book, the Boss stated only who lived in which tent. But it
was lost on no one even then how well calculated his assignments
were. For himself, he took a small pole tent and three tent mates.
He went against every human instinct to avoid unpleasant people
and to fight those who challenged his authority. First Officer
Greenstreet wrote about Shackleton's tent picks: "He collected
with him the ones he thought wouldn't mix with the others. They
were not so easy to get on with, the ones he had in his tent with
him—they were quite a mixed bag."

One choice was the photographer Frank Hurley. Hurley was
clever and strong and had the potential to be a rival power for the
men's loyalty. As it was, he had several secret conversations with
Macklin sharply critical of some of Shackleton's orders. Macklin
hinted at them in his diary, writing some sections in code. Shackle-

ton identified Hurley's big ego as his vulnerable spot, and so made the photographer feel he was his adviser and confidante. The more Hurley got to know the Boss, the more he liked him. He wrote after living with him for two weeks: "Have great admiration for the boss, who is very considerate and kindly disposed, and an excellent comrade."

Shackleton's other choice was Hubert Hudson, the navigating officer, whom he worried would be hard to live with because he was so argumentative. Shackleton kept him busy debating various topics. Conversation inside the tent was at turns lively and intimate.

The physicist Reginald James was anxious, and by taking him in his tent, Shackleton was able to make him feel more secure. "He was an excellent tent-mate & once inside the tent dropped to a very large extent the commander," James said in an interview later.

> We had great discussions about all manner of things. One of his great arguments was in favor of "practical" scientific research as against pure. He had, or said he had, little use for pure science and thought our efforts should be directed to practical lines. I used to take the other view & we would argue at length but never get anywhere.
>
> Sometimes he would be reminiscent and these times were most enjoyable, for he had met many people from kings down and told a tale well, and had a sense of the humor of the situation. He would discuss new expeditions, not only polar, hidden treasures, schemes of all kinds for getting rich quickly, & one would realize what a gambler he was. Or he would read or recite poetry & then one would see a different side of him. One of his favorite amusements was the game known as "animal, mineral or vegetable," in which one of the players has to guess some object agreed upon by the rest by asking questions to which the only answer allowed is "yes" or "no." Shackleton had quite an uncanny skill at this game. By a few judicious questions he would narrow down the field of inquiry & rapidly arrive at the answer however remote the thing might be.

In tent No. 2, a small hoop tent, he put his trusted colleague Frank Wild. The Boss paired him with James McIlroy because he knew Wild had become very fond of the worldly, sardonic surgeon. Wordie was added, possibly because he needed some cheering up at the time. The Boss also wanted Wild to handle Harry McNeish, a pessimistic and unhappy person he wanted isolated from the more impressionable young men.

In tent No. 3, a large hoop tent, Shackleton assigned all the seamen. They had been living together since the start of the expedition and had grown close. The tent held Walter How, William Bakewell, William Stephenson, Ernest Holness, Timothy McCarthy, Thomas McLeod, John Vincent, and the cook, Charles Green.

In tent No. 4, a small hoop tent, he put Tom Crean, Alfred Cheetham, Leonard Hussey, and George Marston. It was a pleasant group. Crean was a natural leader, always reliable and hardworking. Cheetham was another hard-working and popular crewman. Hussey, twenty-one years old, was a comic and his banjo playing, as Shackleton predicted, was enjoyed by all. He and Marston, the artist, didn't like to do any extra work, but they carried their load.

Tent No. 5, a large pole tent, was crowded with Frank Worsley, Robert Clark, Lionel Greenstreet, Thomas Orde-Lees, A. J. Kerr, Louis Rickinson, Alexander Macklin, and Perce Blackborow, the stowaway. The men thought that Shackleton surely had slipped in putting that tent together; Clark noted that it had "all the ingredients of gunpowder." Kerr, Rickinson, and Blackborow were mild mannered. But Worsley was erratic and unpredictable, Macklin had a temper, Greenstreet and Orde-Lees tended to get on people's nerves, and Clark had a constant sniff that drove people crazy. To everyone's surprise, the men bonded despite occasional tension. Orde-Lees wrote, "We really get on wonderfully well considering the way that we are constantly and literally treading upon one another's toes."

Shackleton made sure everyone knew what to do in case the ice broke up under the tents. Each person was given a post and a duty. The Boss held emergency drills: He blew his whistle and the men would pack their gear and provisions and take down the tents and get ready to move. Otherwise, Shackleton kept life as normal as possible—with prompt meals, set duties, and daily exercise. Hurley outlined the camp routine as follows: "Camp arise at 8 A.M., breakfast 8:30. . . . Routine duties viz seal scouting, tidying camp, etc. till 1 P.M. Lunch variable. . . . Afternoon is spent at individual's discretion, reading walking, etc. Generally seal or penguin hoosh at 5:30 P.M., and cocoa. Turn into sleeping bags immediately after. Take an hour's watch each alternate night."

The dogs still had to be exercised daily. The men also took turns as tent "peggy," fetching meals for the rest of the tent from the cook's stove in the makeshift galley. Of course, Shackleton had a library set up—in the galley, which also held a workspace for Hurley and Marston. The men spent time mending their tents and smoothing paths. Most important, the carpenter McNeish was building up the sides of the lifeboats for the crew's inevitable flight from the increasingly unstable floe. Hunting parties went out daily, when weather permitted. In bad weather, they sewed clothes or boots and played cards.

Shackleton made sure the men
didn't lose their sense of humor.

The Boss provided plenty of diversions, especially when inclement weather kept the men in their tents for days on end. Hurley recalled that when the crew retrieved Worsley's captain's uniform from the *Endurance,* Shackleton donned the hat and sword and strutted for everyone. He visited every tent every day, only missing visits when he had such severe sciatica that he couldn't leave his sleeping bag without help. "This was the only time while we were on the floe that he failed to visit each tent, even during blizzards, to make enquiries as to every man's health and comfort," Wild remembered.

The Boss also sent Leonard Hussey from tent to tent with his banjo to engage all the men in sing-alongs. "He was a very good performer and on Saturday nights we continued to hold the usual concert; unaccompanied now by liquid refreshment," said Wild. Otherwise, the men dropped in on each other in the tents. Wild and McIlroy seemed to be popular guests. Hurley wrote on December 2 of a concert held in his tent with Wild, Wordie, and McIlroy: "A very pleasant evening was spent and many old favorites rendered by Hussey's banjo." Again on December 18, Wild and McIlroy were invited over. Macklin wrote about the same time that Wild and McIlroy came into tent No. 5 for a sing-along and Hussey brought his banjo. "We had a merry evening, though it is difficult to find songs that we have not heard many times before," Macklin wrote.

The doctor also mentioned "a craze for Bridge amongst members of the tent and Sir E. and McIlroy and others have been in, giving advice and instruction. All smoked strong tobacco; so strong that Rickinson and I were almost overpowered and had to leave the tent—I with a severe headache."

Cards were only popular when it was relatively warm, as it was almost impossible to deal them with gloves on. Hurley and the Boss for weeks played several games of poker for winnings they would collect when they returned home—theater tickets, shaving cases, wine, collar boxes, and a hat from "Johnson, 38 Bond Street, Hatler"—certain they would get there eventually.

The one thing that always cheered up the men was a good, plentiful meal, and Shackleton used rations to lift morale. The young men, at least, were always hungry. The older men, because of their age and their survival experiences, could do with less food, and sometimes gave part of their share to the younger men. The one exception was Worsley, who at forty had the appetite of someone half his age.

Shackleton forced the men to let go of the
past and focus on what they needed to survive.

On the evening of November 21, Shackleton was out for a walk on the floe when a sudden movement of the ship caught his eye. It had been a month since she had been abandoned. But during that time the *Endurance* served as a storage depot, the repository of tons of food and supplies. Shackleton yelled out to the men, and everyone turned out to watch the ship from a distance. It must have been a heartbreaking sight to see the beautiful ship break apart. For more than a year it had been their home—one they had grown very fond of—and it had been their last link to civilization. Macklin recalled the Boss's reaction: "As always with him, what had happened had happened; it was in the past and he looked to the future. . . . Without emotion, melodrama or excitement he said, 'Ship and stores have gone, so now we'll go home.'"

Shackleton never wasted time or energy lamenting things that had passed or that he couldn't change. "A man must shape himself to a new mark directly the old one goes to ground," he said. His intolerance of waste gave him a certain efficiency in his work that some mistook for impatience or ruthlessness. He didn't waste questions in interviews; he didn't waste time making empty gestures; he didn't waste energy disciplining people for no reason. Any spare time he had was spent reading and planning. If he took a step, it was to reach a goal; if he gave an order, it was necessary for survival.

Shackleton's motto was "Prospice," meaning "look forward." It was the title of a Robert Browning poem that his wife Emily often quoted to him:

> *No! let me taste the whole of it, fare like my peers*
> *   The heroes of old,*
> *Bear the brunt, in a minute pay life's glad arrears*
> *   Of pain, darkness and cold.*

For sudden the worst turns the best to the brave,
  The black minute's at end . . .

For all their monumental problems, the diarists among the men
wrote often of their happiness. Dr. Macklin wrote on December 8,
"It is an anxious time for us, but everybody is cheerful and bright.
We are getting a good allowance of food, and we have adapted ourselves pretty well to this tent life. I feel just as happy here as I did
when I was in hospital with all the comforts, large rooms of my
own, bathroom and all conveniences etc. If we come through alive
and safe it will be a great experience to look back on."

Shackleton sought out advice,
but made final decisions alone.

The Boss asked all the men what they thought of any important situation. He was keeping his finger on the pulse of the crew, letting
them have their say, and collecting ideas. "That was the big difference between him and Scott. Scott was much too Navy," James
told Shackleton's biographers, the Fishers. Shackleton "did a lot of
thinking out loud in the tent but his decisions were definitely his
own."

Greenstreet could attest to that. Shackleton once asked him how
he thought things were going. "Well sir, I don't think it would be a
bad idea if every seal and penguin came up we killed and depoted,
and made a cache of food," Greenstreet replied. But that wasn't
what the Boss had decided: "Oh, you're a bloody pessimist. That
would put the wind up the foc'sle crowd; they'd think we were
never going to get out." In fact, it made the men more nervous not
to stockpile food.

Orde-Lees was good-natured about being humored by Shackleton. On December 20, he wrote, the Boss called him into his tent
and "informed me confidentially that he had it in mind to make an
effort to march to the west" to Paulet Island. "It was not long a secret," Orde-Lees said in what could only have been feigned naiveté,

"for by the time I had walked over to our tent there was a general buzz of pleasurable anticipation around the camp."

The Boss, however, wasn't above obeying the wishes of his men. Orde-Lees wrote some months before on the ship that when an exhausted Shackleton said he was skipping dinner, he advised him to go to the dinner table so that the men might feel better, and Shackleton obliged.

Shackleton made sure everyone felt he was doing something worthwhile to get out of the situation.

On December 20, the Boss assembled the entire group and explained his plans: The men would drag two boats to Paulet Island, making more than two miles a day, marching at night when the floe surface was harder. They would sleep during the day when it was warm. The march was pointless, but the men were getting restless. Shackleton knew he had to keep them busy and silence those still insisting that more could be done. It gave them a feeling of being in control of their own destiny.

"There is a psychological aspect to the question also," Shackleton wrote about the march. "It will be much better for the men in general to feel that even though progress is slow they are on their way to land than it will be simply to sit down and wait for the tardy north-westerly drift to take us out of this cruel waste of ice. We will make an attempt to move."

He had applied the same psychology on the first march, and even ten months earlier when the ship first got stuck. Then he had the crew attempt to pick, saw, and ram their way out of a sea of thick ice in which they were trapped. Shackleton didn't want anyone to feel that something wasn't tried that might have worked. The psychological benefit of any action, however, was always weighed against its practicality.

The decision to haul the boats meant Christmas would have to be celebrated early, on the twenty-second. The crew had a feast made up of the luxuries that couldn't be taken on the boats.

The men went to sleep and got up at 3 A.M. to sledge the *James Caird* and the *Dudley Docker*. The two lifeboats were moved in succession. The Boss, Wordie, Hussey, and Hudson led the effort by forging a path. Fifteen men in harnesses dragging one boat followed them. The dogs then transported additional supplies. After all advanced about half a mile, they stopped and went back to get the other boat. Worsley and Wild were in charge of the men doing the hauling. The march was backbreaking and tedious and the ice difficult to traverse. Because of the relays, the haulers had to trudge three miles to advance just one.

Christmas fell on the third day of the march. "We wondered, too, that day, as we sat down to our 'lunch' of stale, thin bannock and a mug of thin cocoa, what they were having at home," the Boss wrote, perhaps exaggerating the skimpiness of the meal. "All hands were very cheerful. The prospect of a relief from the monotony of life on the floe raises our spirits."

Macklin wrote in his diary: "It's a hard, rough, jolly life."

Not everyone found it so jolly. On December 27, after five days of hauling, McNeish got fed up. He "refused to obey Worsley's orders, using at the same time abusive language," Macklin wrote. Shackleton was furious about the threat to group discipline. Immediately, he pulled McNeish aside to explain in no uncertain terms that he was to obey orders. That night, in camp, he called all hands and read the ship's articles. Although the ship had sunk, the contract declared, the entire crew was under the command of the officers while on the floe. That also meant, he assured them, that they would be paid for their work until they were back home.

That move isolated and ended any mutinous tendencies. Shackleton would write of the situation only this: "Everyone working well except the carpenter [McNeish]: I shall never forget him in this time of strain & stress." He did not forget, or forgive.

After days of backbreaking effort the crew had managed to advance only seven and a half miles, and the boats were getting battered. Sir Ernest calculated it would take them three hundred days to reach the land to the west. That was, of course, an absurdly long time. Shackleton had proved his point. There was nothing to do but to stop and set up a camp, to the disappointment of many who appreciated the hard work. Shackleton wrote in his diary: "Put footstep of courage into stirrup of patience."

Shackleton did what was hardest at the time: nothing.

The men's new home was called Patience Camp. They would stay there for more than three months. Any further action would have been wasted energy at this point. As the brief Antarctic summer wound down, Shackleton prepared for the planned boat trip to land. "Waiting. waiting. waiting," he wrote.

The time dragged by. It was much harder to keep up the men's spirits now. This camp was austere, lacking any of the hominess of Ocean Camp. They had left behind most of the supplies that had made their lives comparatively pleasant. The blustery weather and mushy surface ice were such that at times the men couldn't even stand upright; they had to crawl to the galley to get meals. The men began to spend a lot of time in their tents. Macklin wrote that when the weather was at its worst he didn't even undress at nights so as to be ready to jump into the boat when necessary. He only changed his socks. "All other gear has to dry on my body as it gets wet," he wrote. He then added with the optimism that had come to characterize the expedition: "Still one cannot grumble—I am in the Antarctic with my eyes open, and I feel it is up to me to help pull myself out of it again."

Some of the men, however, were beginning to despair. Frank Worsley, for instance, had become depressed in March and stopped talking, which was very unusual for him. Even Dr. Macklin became angry with Shackleton, calling him a child and an imbecile in one coded part of his diary.

As 1915 came to a close, Shackleton wrote of his wish for the new year: "May the new one bring us good fortune a safe deliverance from this anxious time & all good things to those we love so far away . . . Reading Babylon & Assyria out of E.B. [*Encyclopaedia Britannica*]. Ice seems to be rotting away. Thinking much makes one not desirous of writing much. . . . I long for some rest free from thought, but thank God all are well & fit & safe."

McNeish was less nostalgic. He wrote in his diary on January 1: "New Years Day, which we celebrate in Scotland with cake & wine, while we are celebrating it here afloat on the Antarctic ice floes not knowing what way we will drift next or be frozen in for another winter."

Shackleton prepared the men for
unpopular orders by giving warnings far in advance.

The Boss liked to float rumors and ideas ahead of time when a difficult decision had to be made. It gave the men time to mull over the idea of a plan before having to deal with the reality of it. Shackleton talked for some time about the dogs' drain on supplies. On January 14, he had Wild shoot four teams. Hurley was allowed to keep his team two days longer to retrieve more stores from Ocean Camp. When it was time for his dogs to be shot, Hurley accepted it as "a sad but unfortunate necessity," considering how much food the dogs consumed. Shackleton left the task to Wild while he spent the afternoon with Hurley, taking him for a long walk to keep his mind off the matter.

Shackleton's gesture was reminiscent of the time he had kept Hurley company while the photographer went through the depressing exercise of thinning out his negatives. Hurley had taken more than 500 photographs since the start of the expedition, but knew he had to lighten his load after they abandoned ship. Shackleton sat with him on the ice and helped him edit his collection down to 120 glass-plate negatives. Hurley smashed the ones he didn't keep so he wouldn't be tempted to second-guess himself. He kept just a Kodak pocket camera and two rolls of film for the rest of the expedition.

On January 21, when the men drifted across the Antarctic Circle, they celebrated with a good meal. The men also wanted to celebrate the Boss's birthday on February 15 but Shackleton forbid it out of fear of wasting precious food. He could see the men needed a special event though, and so they celebrated Leap Year Day, honoring "the escape of some of our bachelors from the Fair Sex."

The men were still killing seals, but the animals were getting scarce as the polar autumn advanced. In addition to skimpier meals, the shortage of seals meant a lack of blubber for the stove. At one point, Shackleton had to limit hot drinks to one a day.

One such drink would stick out in the minds of many of the men. The Boss, at Worsley's insistence, retrieved the third lifeboat, the *Stancomb Wills,* from Ocean Camp. On February 2 he decided it was safe to send eighteen men under Wild to get the boat, which had drifted to within two miles. Still, it was a grueling task. As the exhausted group returned, Shackleton sledged out to greet them with pannikins of hot tea.

Not long after that, the ice began to break up. Orde-Lees served as an early warning signal, as he was prone to seasickness and reacted to the slightest increase in movement. Wild, who had more experience than the others with pack ice, was wary of launching the boats. He dreaded the "masses of ice weighing hundreds to thousands of tons heaving up and down and churning against each other with a continuous thundering roar, making it exceedingly dangerous to enter or leave even with a well-built wooden ship specially constructed for the purpose. How much more hazardous then to escape with three frail boats."

At 11 A.M. on April 9, a crack ripped through the camp. The men finally had a chance to escape into open water before another polar winter set in and again choked the area around them with ice. When the lead opened wide, the men quickly launched the boats. "Our home was being shattered under our feet," Shackleton wrote, "and we had a sense of loss and incompleteness hard to describe."

SHACKLETON'S WAY
OF GETTING THE GROUP THROUGH A CRISIS

- When crisis strikes, immediately address your staff. Take charge of the situation, offer a plan of action, ask for support, and show absolute confidence in a positive outcome.

- Get rid of unnecessary middle layers of authority. Direct leadership is more efficient in emergency situations.

- Plan several options in detail. Get a grasp of the possible consequences of each, always keeping your eye on the big picture.

- Streamline supplies and operations so they won't slow you down.

- Give your staff an occasional reality check to keep them on course. After time, people will start to treat a crisis situation as business as usual and lose their focus.

- Keep your malcontents close to you. Resist your instinct to avoid them and instead try to win them over and gain their support.

- Defuse tension. In high-stress situations use humor to put people at ease, and keep your staff busy.

- Let go of the past. Don't waste time or energy regretting past mistakes or fretting over what you can't change.

- Ask for advice and information from a variety of sources, but ultimately make decisions based on your own best judgment.

- Let all the people involved in the crisis participate in the solution, even if that means doling out some work that is less than vital.

- Be patient. Sometimes the best course of action is to do nothing but watch and wait.

- Give your staff plenty of time to get used to the idea of an unpopular decision.

WORKING IT IN

Jeremy Larken, managing director of OCTO Ltd., a crisis-management company based in Chester, England, uses Shackleton's example of leadership in the midst of turmoil in his seminars for senior executives. Mr. Larken particularly likes to review for his clients the Boss's actions in the days after the men had to abandon ship. "I do it to give them a role model for how people should behave in a raw crisis: with rationality, optimism, and clarity of mind—particularly with a clear objective in view," he says.

Most of Mr. Larken's work involves preparing top executives and their crisis-management teams for a wide variety of problems, from incidents demanding immediate remedy, such as nuclear-power-plant emergencies, to any number of longer-term corporate crises. He and his senior colleagues also advise companies on drawing up realistic corporate-risk profiles.

Mr. Larken points out that high-level managers tend to be very competent at their day-to-day business—they have to be to rise as far as they have. They are not, however, always good at handling a unique and rapidly unfolding crisis, when they have to respond immediately and with only limited information. "A lot of managers assume that crisis is ordinary business accelerated, but you need to organize quite differently and set up different communication," he says.

Mr. Larken has been a lifelong fan of Shackleton, and for good reason—he is part of the family. Born Edmund Shackleton Jeremy Larken, he "grew up in the Shackleton culture," he says. He was educated at Bryanston, a progressive school in Dorset, England, and has been reading books about the explorer since he was a child. His mother, Peggy Shackleton, born in 1908, is a cousin of Sir Ernest. She still recalls as a young girl going to hear Sir Ernest speak about his breathtaking experiences on the *Nimrod* expedition and meeting him afterward. As an adult, she grew increasingly enamored of the explorer's story and her family's mixed

Anglo-Irish-Quaker heritage. In midlife, she returned to her family's Quaker roots, and to her maiden name, to write books and commentary.

Mr. Larken began researching Shackleton as a leadership model in the early 1990s when he set up OCTO. Now, he sees Shackleton as an outstanding example of how to handle the several phases of a typical crisis-response model, as Mr. Larken has drawn it. Those phases include immediate assessment and action, deep assessment of key issues, setting objectives and sighting opportunities, and stepping back from center stage to let employees continue the work while continuing to inspire and nurture the team.

To begin making a proper assessment, managers have to get over one of the toughest hurdles: letting go of the past. That is, they must let go of familiar work routines and let go of obsessive ruminations—often denial—about how they got into their mess.

In a crisis, Shackleton never held onto emotional baggage. "The thing I particularly admire him for is his ability to refocus unerringly on actuality," Mr. Larken says. "He was brilliant at turning people around and making them see the new situation."

He likes Dr. Macklin's description of how Shackleton handled the sinking of the *Endurance:* "As always with him, what had happened had happened. It was in the past and he looked to the future."

Another stumbling block for managers, Mr. Larken adds, is dealing with setting objectives. He and one of his partners in OCTO were once invited by a major nuclear-power company in England to report on a high-level emergency exercise. When Mr. Larken's colleague asked several managers individually to explain their objectives in the planned operation, they gave widely varying responses. "Even the most able people often can't get their minds around or clearly state an objective in a crisis situation," Mr. Larken says. Or worse, "they only grope and grasp the obvious."

That's when he brings out the example of Shackleton, who could always articulate clearly the next step of his plans. The Boss consistently had his strategy right, while keeping it under constant review, Mr. Larken says.

Mr. Larken followed his father into the British Royal Navy and spent thirty-three years there. His seminars often draw on his experience as a commander of the headquarters amphibious-assault ship during the Falkland Islands conflict in 1982. Afterward, he became a two-star admiral, managing U.K. military support outside the NATO area and heading crisis operations for the U.K. Ministry of Defense.

In 1991, he retired from the navy at the age of fifty-two and formed OCTO. It was then that he began to delve more deeply into Shackleton's qualities, placing them in the context of commercial leadership. When Mr. Larken briefs his clients, he sometimes uses a quick comparative sketch of Shackleton, Scott, and Amundsen, to point to Shackleton's unique strengths. For Scott: ambitious, naïve technically, hierarchical, arrogant, wary of colleagues more able than himself, indifferent selector, poor trainer, bad safety record, a gifted author. Amundsen: single-minded, objective, meticulous technically and as a planner, good safety record, formidable but not charismatic, realistic, lonely, supreme achiever. For Shackleton: single-minded, excelled in crisis, technically sensible but not innovative, gregarious, excellent public speaker, broadly objective, good conceptual planner, effective selector and trainer, good safety record, erratic in business, bored by administration, politically astute.

Like his famous relative, Mr. Larken has developed the skills of a good listener, allowing himself to empathize with the speaker. He has long honed memory techniques so he can speak to people "in a genuine context of their personal interests and concerns," he says. He advises managers even of large organizations to get to know well as many of their employees as possible. They, in turn, will spread a positive image of their leader among the wider group. When Mr. Larken was a senior naval officer, for example, he had the very Shackletonian habit of showing up at 4 A.M. to have tea with the machinist on duty.

He also suggests executives build trust by following Shackleton's example of being "genuinely and demonstratively considerate of your team's welfare—and consistently so." A trusted leader will find a staff willing to support almost any decision.

Mr. Larken has had the opportunity to follow many careers and train many people. He says he often has been amazed to watch an individual grow into a real leader. "We can all learn about leadership like we can learn about everything else," he says. Even those we perceive as being born with charisma and talent have to work at being leaders, he adds.

"The onset of crisis is too late to decide to become an effective leader; the process must be a perennial and cumulative part of each manager's personal development plan and practice," Mr. Larken tells his clients. "The sooner this is started as a systematic process, the better, but now is probably not too late."

Any executive, he says, can learn much from Shackleton.

6

FORMING TEAMS FOR TOUGH ASSIGNMENTS

He didn't care if he went without a shirt on his own back, so long as the men he was leading had sufficient clothing. He was a wonderful man in that way; you thought the party mattered more than anything else.

—Lionel Greenstreet, first officer, *Endurance*

Royal Geographical Society, London

SAFE LANDING

Shackleton's crew arrived safely on Elephant Island after nearly a week in three small lifeboats, struggling against roiling, ice-filled seas. The Boss had brilliantly balanced the talents, experience, and personalities of his men, creating three efficient crews that could withstand a grueling test of the limits of their abilities.

FINALLY UNDER WAY IN THE BOATS, SHACKLETON'S GROUP headed west. Within a radius of some one hundred miles lay the Antarctic Peninsula and several of the South Shetland Islands. Whaling stations were sprinkled throughout those islands closest to the peninsula, and the men hoped they could either make it to the stations or land in a place where they had a good chance of being spotted by a passing ship. About sixty miles to the northeast was Elephant Island. The prevailing winds and currents might have easily carried them there, but it was so remote it would be unlikely that a ship would pass by close enough to see their signal. Paulet Island, of course, was attractive for its stores of food. Best of all, Shackleton reasoned, would be Deception Island, where there was a whaling station.

At this point, the men were willing to accept just about any piece of land. They hadn't set foot on solid ground since December 5, 1914, and it was April 9, 1916. They started this latest journey under overcast skies, in temperatures hovering around 20 degrees Fahrenheit.

In launching the lifeboats, Shackleton had to organize the men into three tough, self-reliant units that would be strong enough to get through the task ahead. He used the same careful balancing act to assign boat crews that he had used for the tents, but with a different focus. Shackleton's tent selection was about keeping up morale and damping down dissent. The boat assignments were much more critical. Each crew faced an extraordinary challenge, both mental and physical, that could mean life or death. Their task was made all the more difficult by the fact that the three boats were very different in terms of their seaworthiness.

The *James Caird,* 22.5 feet long and 6 feet wide, was a double-ended whaler and by far the best of the three lifeboats. The boat "did magnificently under sail," Macklin wrote. Its sides were built up to a height of 3 feet 7 inches and it was decked over at both ends by McNeish, a brilliant carpenter despite his disagreeable nature. He used Marston's paints to seal the seams. The raised sides kept out the spray while under sail, but made rowing awkward.

The *Dudley Docker* was a Norwegian-built boat, 22 feet long and 6 feet wide with a hull that was 3 feet deep. It was a cutter, flat at the stern and fairly sturdy.

The *Stancomb Wills,* another Norwegian-built cutter, was the smallest and least seaworthy of the lifeboats. It was 20 feet 8 inches long and 5.5 feet wide. Its hull was only 27 inches high so when fully loaded it was a mere 17 inches above the water line, guaranteeing that it would be constantly flooded. It was also heavy for its size and hard to row and sail. The men called it the *Stinking Willy.* It seemed inevitable that it would have to be towed. Shackleton didn't want to use it at first, but realized he needed it for the extra space and so retrieved it from Ocean Camp at the last minute. Being able to carry so many more provisions greatly widened the margin of safety for the group.

Again, the Boss didn't reveal even in his diaries how he thought through his deft crew assignments for the boats. With few exceptions, he avoided any public discussion of the flaws and foibles of his crew or colleagues in exploration. For years afterward, however, crew members marveled at his masterly way of mixing experience, talent, and temperament into efficient units, all the while being sensitive to rank and position. For the boats, Shackleton aimed to make each one a complete unit that could survive on its own, should it come to that. Each had a solid core of crewmen: an accomplished navigator, a couple of good seamen, and someone to administer medical care. The other spaces were then filled mostly according to personality.

***Shackleton headed the best and biggest boat
and picked the weakest crewmen to accompany him.***

The *James Caird* carried eleven in all. As usual, Shackleton kept both the troublemakers and the troubled close by. He took the two toughest cases: Vincent and McNeish, both pessimists. He could keep an eye on them and keep them from demoralizing others on what promised to be a very difficult journey. He also took the scientists, all relatively inexperienced at sea: Hussey, Clark, Wordie, and James. Being close to the Boss gave them a sense of security and also ensured that they weren't a burden to other lifeboats. Shackleton also took Green, the cherished cook, and the resourceful Hurley, who needed to have the Boss's ear, but was also apt to issue orders of his own if placed with the gullible young men.

Others in this group were the Boss's trusted No. 2, Frank Wild, who would underpin the crew and help keep an eye on everyone, and McCarthy, a cheerful, competent seaman who would surely carry his own weight as a sailor and be impervious to the grumbling of Vincent and McNeish. For the boat's doctor, Shackleton chose Hussey, who wasn't a physician, but had some medical training. In fact, Hussey went on to become a doctor after the expedition.

Shackleton put together a dependable crew that
would be a strong middle link to the weakest element.

The *Dudley Docker* had far and away the strongest crew—nine in all. Shackleton figured he needed one boatload of strong sailors whom he could count on to take care of the inferior *Stancomb Wills* while his hands were full. He was determined that all the boats make it together. Frank Worsley, an excellent navigator and expert at sailing small boats, led the *Docker* crew. The others included the artist Marston, who had experience in the region; the surgeon Macklin, who grew up "on the end of an oar" in the Scilly Islands off southern England where his father was a doctor; and the six experienced seamen—Greenstreet, Cheetham, Orde-Lees, Holness, Kerr, and McLeod. McLeod, in his fifties, was considered the best sailor of the entire *Endurance* crew.

Shackleton chose the workhorses
for the toughest assignment.

Hudson led the unfortunate *Stancomb Wills*. He was not a strong leader, but he was the *Endurance*'s navigating officer and Shackleton would not usurp his power. He did, however, place next to Hudson the stalwart Tom Crean. The surgeon on board was McIlroy. This lifeboat carried just eight but they were experienced and solid sailors: Chief Engineer Rickinson, and four seamen—Blackborow, How, Bakewell, and Stephenson. The seamen were hard workers who could get a job done with few complaints, and that's just what Shackleton needed for this assignment.

The first day out, the boats made little progress. The crews of the *Dudley Docker* and the *James Caird* had started out carrying some sledges but quickly abandoned that idea. The sea was a churning, foaming tide of icy debris. Worse, the boats were caught between two huge masses of ice that were converging. It took an incredible amount of exertion for any of the crews, especially the one on the *Stancomb Wills,* to stay ahead of the rush. Had they been caught in the convergence, they would have been doomed. "It was an unusual and startling experience," Shackleton wrote with great understatement.

Shackleton trusted his team leaders
but always kept an eye on each individual.

For the first night in the boats, the men were fortunate in finding a large floe on which to pitch their tents. While the rest slept, Shackleton kept quiet watch. Ever since the *Endurance* had gotten stuck in January 1915, he had taken bottom-line responsibility for the life, health, and safety of every one of his men. Back in August, on the ship, Orde-Lees wrote, "I know for a fact that he did not once lie down for three days & I don't think he has undressed for ten days. Even when he did condescend to rest a little, it was only for about three hours at a time. . . . He seems always on the alert, especially at night, having certainly been up every night for the last three weeks."

Sleep was to become an increasingly rare luxury for the Boss. His ceaseless vigilance would save a life that night of April 9, 1916, which happened to be his twelfth wedding anniversary. The Boss had been in his sleeping bag only about an hour when he got up to survey the floe. As he approached the seamen's tent in the dark, an unexpectedly large swell tossed the floe and it split under the men's tent. Someone yelled, "Crack!" and one man hit the water, letting out a yelp. Shackleton quickly threw himself onto the edge of the ice, and as the others watched, he heaved the man and his sleeping bag back onto the floe. The seaman, Holness, seemed more annoyed than grateful. When asked if he was all right, he replied, "Yes, but I lost a ——— tin of 'baccy," Wild later wrote, omitting the expletive. When someone suggested he should be thankful the Boss had saved him, Holness snapped: "So I am, but that doesn't bring the tobacco back."

The men abandoned any notion of rest that night. Some walked Holness to keep his blood circulating. Hudson gave him some dry—or at least drier—clothing. Others began moving all the gear to one side of the crack so nothing would get separated and lost. Suddenly, the gap opened wide, stranding Shackleton on the other side. He was soon out of sight. Wild launched a boat and retrieved him. As typical after a trauma, Shackleton had the cook serve warm milk and gave his men a treat they hadn't opened yet on the expedition: some Streimers Polar Nut Food, a nougat rolled in nuts that the men came to love.

At daybreak on the tenth, the men again took to the lifeboats under cloudy skies. It was clear by now that these vessels were taking in too much water in the rough seas, overloaded as they were with food and supplies. The *Caird* carried nearly 4 tons; the *Docker* had 1.5 tons; and the *Wills* had 1.25 tons. The crews had to leave behind gear: wood, harnesses, skis, cooking utensils, and dried vegetables. Once unburdened, the wind carried the *Caird* and *Docker* easily over the bumpy water, but the rag of a sail on the *Wills* left it struggling to keep up. It fell far behind and had to be rescued. Again that night, they found a safe place on the floes to rest.

The morning of the eleventh was again overcast and felt particularly gloomy. "It was a day that seemed likely to lead to no more days," Shackleton wrote in *South*. "I do not think I had ever before felt the anxiety that belongs to leadership quite so keenly."

Their troubles had begun the night before. It had started to snow and the wind had picked up. In the predawn darkness, a large chunk of the floe had dropped into the sea and the men had to move their provisions out to a safer spot. Much worse was the realization, in the morning light, that their floe had joined itself to the pack ice. They were trapped again, about 100 yards away from open water. The sea was churning, but all the men could do was watch. "We waited and waited, hour by hour, watching the wonderful conflict of the elements, at times unmindful of our desperate position, spellbound by the imposing majesty of the spectacle," wrote Orde-Lees.

The sea was violently undulating under the ice. One minute the men would find themselves at the crest of a wave, then the next they dropped into a valley, with twelve-foot swells on either side. The little floe they were standing on was getting smaller and smaller, ground down by all the motion and splashed by heavy waves. When the men finally saw a channel of water, they jumped into the boats and threaded their way through the ice. It was after-noon before they were clear of it. Dusk came around 5 P.M. but the crews had to keep going. There would be no camping on the floes at night. The *Docker* began serving food, and finally the *Caird* put the amazingly agile Green atop a floe to cook up some hoosh and milk for everyone. The men drank it down scalding hot to get some warmth into their bellies. To further lighten their loads, they threw overboard the heavy iron from the hoop tents. Little by little, they were losing the few remaining items that brought the slightest comfort.

With the darkness of the evening came bitter cold and driving sleet. Every piece of equipment, and the men themselves, became encased in a thick layer of ice as the sleet and spray froze over them. Their oars became impossibly slippery. The wind went right to their bones as their trusted Burberry suits became soaked. They occasionally had to take off their mittens to wring out the water; even wet gloves spared their fingers from frostbite. Some refused to sleep, choosing instead to continue rowing in an effort to stay warm.

Unnerving them further, a school of killer whales surrounded them, blowing "blood-curdling blasts," as one man described it. They were terrified that the animals would emerge from the water, toss aside a boat, and feed on them. What's more, several men be-came seasick in the turbulent waters.

For the next hundred hours, none of them got much rest.

Some relief came on April 12. The day started brightly, and even in their desperation, the men couldn't help noticing the beautiful effect of the sunlight tinting purple the heaving hills of ice on the water. Shackleton pulled up alongside the *Dudley Docker* and jumped in to consult the charts with Worsley. It was more bad news. Unbelievably, although they were heading west with all their might, the current had pushed them thirty miles east of Patience Camp! They expected Shackleton to be furious. Instead, he kept his composure.

They turned west again. "Sir Ernest led the way in the *James Caird* and showed great skill in getting along," Macklin wrote. The others were struggling. The *Wills* had to be towed by the *Docker* for two hours. That night, they had to tie the three little boats together for security and moor them to a floe. The men hunkered down for the night, soaked with spray and snow. Shackleton shouted to the men through the darkness to offer encouragement and check their status. "The men always managed to reply cheerfully," he wrote.

Shackleton even thought he heard Marston happily singing a sea chanty from the *Docker*. Macklin explained years later in a letter to the author Alfred Lansing: "Lees squeezed Marston out of the only place it was possible to get any sort of comfortable rest, and Marston, in a rage, got up and sat right aft in the stern. He had a good voice and relieved his pent-up feelings by singing song after song. One I particularly remember went 'Twankiedillo, twankiedillo, twankiedillo—dillo—dillo—and a roaring pair of bagpipes made from the green willow!' These songs went away down the wind to the boats tied on astern of us, and next day Shackleton, unaware of the reason, commended Marston for his efforts at keeping the party cheery!"

By the morning of April 13, "the condition of most of the men was pitiable," according to the Boss. They had swollen tongues from lack of water and couldn't choke down any food. The boats were glazed with ice inside and out. During the day, the mild temperatures had softened the surface ice, and the slush made rowing even more difficult. Then a gale kicked up. The men were exhausted, especially those in the *Stancomb Wills,* who had to exert twice the effort of the others to keep up and stay afloat.

Shackleton wasn't afraid to change
his mind as often as the situation dictated.

That day, the Boss faced the inevitable and turned his small flotilla to the northeast toward Elephant Island. It was the fourth time in the four days since taking to the boats that he changed his plans: from heading toward Elephant Island to the east, to aiming for King George Island to the west, to trying for Hope Bay to the southwest (which the men dubbed Hopeless Bay), and back to Elephant Island.

It might have exasperated the weary crew, struggling so hard against huge odds, but Shackleton was certain each time that it was a necessary change, and his men trusted his judgment. James explained years later: "Well-settled plans would suddenly be changed with little warning & a new set made. This was apt to be a little bewildering but it generally turned out to be for the good. This adaptability was one of his strong points. With him it was never a wavering between two ideas. It was a conviction that the second one was a better one & acted accordingly."

Shackleton, attempting to lift the morale of his exhausted men, shouted to Worsley that they make land by the next day. Worsley replied that it was impossible, and for the first time Shackleton snapped at him, worried that his response would demoralize the rest. His patience with Worsley had by now worn thin, perhaps because the captain hadn't been the help to the *Stancomb Wills* that Shackleton had hoped. He took matters into his own hands, and the *Caird* ended up towing the *Wills* toward Elephant Island.

Toward midnight, the boats neared Elephant Island and Worsley offered to look for a landing. They were only twenty miles off the coast, but it was so treacherous they couldn't attempt to land in the dark. Despite efforts to stay together during the night, Shackleton lost sight of the *Docker* and spent some anxious hours worrying about its crew. He took his compass lamp and lit up his icy sail with the light. The *Docker,* spotting his signal, lit a candle under a tent cloth. Shackleton couldn't see the feeble return signal, but Capt. Worsley later wrote that spotting his leader's lighted sail bolstered his determination to catch up. Shackleton was a consistent, visible force at all times, and on this frightening night he was a particular beacon of hope.

"Practically ever since we had first started, Sir Ernest had been standing erect day and night on the stern counter of the *Caird,* only holding on to one of the stays of the little mizzen mast, conning our course the whole time the boats were underway," wrote Orde-Lees. "How he stood the incessant vigil and exposure is marvelous, but he is a wonderful man and so is his constitution. He simply never spares himself if, by his individual toil, he can possibly benefit anyone else."

Shackleton was consistently self-sacrificing. He never let his crewmen go without a comfort that he had it in his power to give.

At one of the stops on the floes, Hurley gave someone his gloves to hold, then jumped into the *Caird* in a quick departure and forgot to retrieve them. Shackleton saw that Hurley had no gloves, took off his own, and thrust them at him. Hurley, tough and uncomplaining, refused, but Shackleton insisted and said he'd throw them overboard if he didn't take them, and the photographer relented. The gesture was typical of the Boss and reminiscent of the one made to Wild on the *Nimrod* expedition years before, when Shackleton threatened to bury his one biscuit in the snow if Wild didn't take it.

The end was now in sight. All hands on the *Dudley Docker* had to furiously bail water to stay afloat on this last leg. Finally, on April 15, Shackleton went ashore on Elephant Island in the *Wills,* having transferred to the boat to help guide it in. The other two boats followed. The men were deliriously happy to be on solid land for the first time in sixteen months. Macklin, in the *Docker,* described the morning they landed: "A bright sun came out and showed up the face of everybody, scarce one of which did not show signs of the night. Some had frostbitten hands and feet, some had lost teeth by some accident; all were white and had heavy rings around the eyes, showing how badly we all needed sleep."

Shackleton wrote in *South* about watching young Rickinson "turn white and stagger" in the surf. He pulled him out of the water and helped him up to the beach. McIlroy later diagnosed heart trouble. "There are some men who will do more than their share of work and who will attempt more than they are physically able to accomplish," Shackleton wrote. "Rickinson was one of these eager souls."

Hudson was in equally bad shape. A tent pole had fallen on him when he was leaving Patience Camp. The injury eventually resulted in a football-size abscess on his hip. He was singled out by others for having a mental breakdown on Elephant Island. In fact, he was probably in agony and dazed by the infection.

Blackborow was also suffering. His feet were frostbitten because he insisted on saving his best boots. Days later, Mr. McIlroy had to amputate all the toes of the stowaway's left foot.

Greenstreet was also in pain from his badly frostbitten hands and foot. He had lost his gloves in the fury of the boat journey and for days after landing couldn't move his fingers. His feet had been soaked and frozen too, but Orde-Lees, in a rare selfless gesture, had put Greenstreet's bad foot against his stomach during the journey and revived it.

The men, who were covered with large saltwater boils from constant wetness and chafing, were too exhausted to unload the boats immediately after landing. Once on shore, most collapsed into sleep. The remarkable Green, however, continued to work. Setting up the stove on a perilous piece of rock, he boiled a big pot of water and served a huge, hot breakfast of powdered milk and seal steaks. "The cook had committed great havoc amongst the seals, slaughtering ten of them with all the primitive savagery of a child killing flies. This was his first opportunity of killing his own larder for himself and he took it with a vengeance," wrote Orde-Lees.

In the end, Green, too, collapsed.

Shackleton pulled the cook down the slope where he had set up his stove and into his own tent and sleeping bag. He decided to replace him with Hurley, whom Shackleton believed needed a new challenge. The others Shackleton bolstered by immediately establishing a manageable routine, but first they slept a long time, taking turns alphabetically for an hour's watch each.

It was Shackleton, of course, who noticed there were high-water marks indicating the beach was swamped at times. The crew would have to move, but the Boss let them stay put for two days to recuperate. The only person Shackleton was relentless with was himself. Although he often pushed his men to near breaking point, he only did so when it was necessary for their survival. He did his best to make sure they had the rest they needed to face any challenge, and that they were well rewarded when they met it.

Shackleton sent Wild and some men to look for a safer place to settle. This reconnaissance party sailed west along the northern shore of the island and after seven miles found a spit of land. Shackleton named it Cape Wild in honor of his valued second in command. The rest of the crew soon followed. Finally, they would have safe ground beneath them. But this long-awaited moment was not what they expected. The spit, like the rest of the island, was covered in penguin guano and was routinely assaulted by blizzards. Elephant Island was stinking, wet, and dangerous. The men were soon calling it Hell-of-an-Island.

Eventually, the men made a shelter by turning two of the boats upside down and setting them atop low walls of stone they had built. The thwarts of the boats served as upper bunks for a lucky few. Otherwise, the men slept like sardines in a can, as they described themselves, lying in rows toe-to-head.

Shackleton knew there was no way they could survive there for long. Surely, they would starve or die of exposure before anyone passed by. They had only five weeks' worth of rations, and the polar winter was about to set in, forming a widening barrier of ice between them and passing seals and penguins. After six months of living outside the ship, the Boss had to admit that there was little more he could do to keep his men together: "The health and mental condition of several men was causing me serious anxiety."

He determined that he and a handful of crewmen would make a bid for South Georgia, eight hundred miles away, as impossible as that sounded. "The risk was justified solely by our urgent need of assistance," he explained.

Everyone set about preparing the *James Caird* for the voyage. McNeish built a covering on the boat using lids from the Venesta packing cases. Bakewell and Greenstreet stitched a cover from sailcloth to make it more waterproof. By April 24, the *Caird* was ready to go.

Shackleton again had to carefully choose his crew for this daring trip. Failure would spell certain doom for everyone.

Shackleton called for volunteers, though he already knew the crew he wanted. He had to consider factors beyond the task at hand—daunting though it was. He also had to think about the consequences for those left stranded on bleak Elephant Island. This time he couldn't take the "old dog" who had supported him at such critical moments in the past. He left Frank Wild to lead the crewmen who would remain behind.

He chose five for the boat. The first pick was obvious: Captain Worsley. Shackleton needed an extraordinary navigator, for if they missed their mark they would be lost in the vast open waters of the South Atlantic. Crean begged to go, and Shackleton saw no reason to leave him behind, making him miserable. He also knew Crean to be tough and levelheaded—qualities that would be particularly valuable on the difficult voyage. The malcontents McNeish and Vincent also were taken. Wild didn't want them poisoning the already grim atmosphere on Elephant Island. McCarthy, whom everyone liked, was selected because he was "a quiet, highly efficient Irishman brought up in sailing ships, and because he never groused or gave any backchat and was a favorite of Worsley," Macklin explained later.

Shackleton told Wild privately that if the *Caird* didn't make it back by the end of August, he should take the *Docker* and try to reach Deception Island. "I practically left the whole situation and scope of action and decision to his own judgment, secure in the knowledge that he would act wisely," Shackleton generously wrote. In fact, the Boss was explicit in his instructions, even deciding that Wild should take Greenstreet and Macklin with him on the trip. Shackleton left nothing to chance during times of crisis.

He tied up other loose ends before departing. He gave Hurley a letter, probably requested by the photographer, that if he didn't survive the boat journey, Hurley got complete control over the "exploitation of all films and photographic reproductions of all negatives taken on this expedition" and would take ownership eighteen months after their first showing. The letter also willed Hurley the Boss's "big binoculars." Vincent witnessed the agreement.

In publicly turning over the reins,
Shackleton left no doubt about his deputy's authority.

When the *James Caird* was ready to set off, Shackleton went ashore to have a very public word with Wild. The gesture made it clear to the others that Wild was going to take his place and that they were being left in very capable hands. Shackleton trusted him to maintain the principles and spirit of the expedition. "All the time I was attending to the boats and watching the condition of the men, Wild sat calmly steering the *Caird,*" Shackleton said of the earlier boat journey to Elephant Island. "He never batted an eyelid. Always the same confident, blue-eyed little man, unmoved by cold or fatigue. He was a tower of strength, as I knew he would be."

As extraordinary as that first boat journey was, it paled in comparison to what was ahead. On the trip to Elephant Island, the men traveled sixty miles in seven days, not counting all the zigzags. The crossing of the South Atlantic to South Georgia would cover eight hundred miles and take seventeen days. Adding to the hardship, the weather had worsened.

Shackleton took thirty days' supply of food for the six men, including sledging rations: cakes of pemmican, nut food, 600 biscuits, 1 case of lump sugar, powdered milk, a tin of bullion cubes, salt, and 36 gallons of water. Ironically, they also took 112 pounds of ice—as a water supply. Gear included instruments: sextant, binoculars, prismatic compass, sea anchor, and charts; and necessities such as paraffin, fuel for the two small stoves, a tin of black seal oil, 6 sleeping bags, some spare clothing, candles, blubber oil, 30 boxes of matches, and 10 boxes of flamers. The men carried the supplies down to the *Caird*. To get heavier items on board, they pushed the boat off shore and used the *Stancomb Wills* to ferry the load. In the rough waves, McNeish and Vincent both were tossed out of the lifeboat. Men rushed out to exchange clothes with them. Curiously, Vincent refused to change his sweater. Eventually it became obvious that he had hidden on his person some of his comrades' discarded valuables and feared exposure. The wet clothes aggravated his rheumatism.

Just before leaving, casks of carefully melted water were finally ferried out; but in the surging surf, one hit the rocks, cracked, and was contaminated with seawater. The *Caird* got off at midday. Shackleton described the heart-rending sight: "The men who were staying behind made a pathetic little group on the beach, with the grim heights of the island behind them and the sea seething at their feet, but they waved to us and gave three hearty cheers. There was hope in their hearts and they trusted us to bring the help that they needed."

More than one man standing on the beach that afternoon thought he had seen the last of their leader. And Shackleton, though forever confident in his own abilities, was deeply concerned that he might return to find that not all of them had made it.

Shackleton never pointed out the weak links in his crew.

Shackleton knew he had at least two negative people on board and perhaps expected that this demanding voyage would take the greatest toll on them. He didn't direct any special warnings toward them, though, so as not to undermine the unity of the whole. Instead, he laid down ground rules that everyone would have to follow. It was typical of Shackleton not to point to the weaknesses of any single man. "Whenever he noticed that a man seemed extra cold and shivered, he would immediately order another hot drink to be served to all. He never let the man know it was on his account, lest he became nervous about himself, and while we all participated it was the coldest, naturally, who got the greatest advantage," Worsley explained.

The first rule of the *Caird* was that there would be no swearing. Everyone had to be positive. Shackleton knew the trip was going to be hell and they had to pull together. The next sixteen days, the Boss said simply, were characterized by "supreme strife amid heaving waters." And his sciatica was flaring up.

Shackleton, as always, established as much order and routine as possible, making sure each man knew what was expected of him. He put three men on watch and three in the sleeping bags, four hours at a time. Of the three on watch, one handled the tiller ropes, one attended the sails, and the third bailed "for all he was worth," Shackleton wrote. Shackleton was wary of the bad blood between McNeish and Worsley because of the carpenter's earlier mutinous episode and so even in the crowded boat he was careful who he had working together. He assigned Worsley to work with his friend McCarthy and rounded out the watch with Vincent. The Boss even orchestrated the changing of the watch so the men wouldn't upset the tiny boat.

Meals were regular. As difficult as it was to use the stoves on board, the men needed hot food for strength and comfort. Meals "were bright beacons in those cold and stormy days," Shackleton said. "The glow of warmth and comfort produced by the food and drink made optimists of us all."

The crew of the *Caird* was weak from being cramped, cold, and hungry. Along with taking regular doses of hot milk, the men did what they could to keep their spirits up. Crean sang. "It was devoid of tune and as monotonous as the chanting of a Buddhist monk at his prayers, yet somehow it was cheerful," Shackleton wrote. "In moments of inspiration Crean would attempt 'The Wearin' o' the Green.'"

There weren't many moments of relief. Layer after layer of ice weighed down the boat and had to be hammered away. One night, Worsley became frozen in one position. The others had to massage and unfold him before they could get him into his sleeping bag. Two of the reindeer-skin sleeping bags had begun to rot. The crew finally tossed them overboard. Shackleton thought it would be preferable, anyway, to keep rotating three, as it was better to climb into a bag already warmed by a body. A fourth bag was kept in case one of the crew had to convalesce for a time. Vincent soon took the extra bag and became incapacitated for the rest of the trip.

The *Caird* yawed continually in huge waves under gray skies. The sea anchor broke off, meaning that someone had to be at the tiller at all times. The crew had to keep the sail up even in gales. The men were in pain. They were frostbitten and developed large blisters on their fingers and hands. Years later, Shackleton would point out the scar on his left hand where a blister broke and the cold had frozen the skin deep in his hand. The men simply ate, treated their frostbite, and hoped to see the next day, the Boss wrote later.

"Each day brought its little round of troubles but also compensation in the form of food and growing hope," Shackleton said. "We felt that we were going to succeed. The odds against us had been great but we were winning through."

Shackleton, however, wrote about one terrifying incident when he was at the tiller. Shortly after midnight on May 5, he called out that there was a clearing sky above, but quickly realized it wasn't a clearing at all. It was the white crest of a huge wave. "During twenty-six years' experience of the ocean in all its moods I had not encountered a wave so gigantic," he said later. "It was a mighty upheaval of the ocean, a thing quite apart from the big white-capped seas that had been our tireless enemy for many days. I shouted, 'For God's sake, hold on! It's got us.'"

Somehow the boat survived, but it was half full of water. The stove was floating; hoosh permeated everything. Grabbing every available container, they bailed for their lives. It took three hours, but they saved the boat and themselves. Shackleton, putting aside any personal feelings, credited McNeish with doing his fair share. Vincent was useless at this point.

The men were low on water and the Boss put them on a ration of eight ounces a day. The water they did have was contaminated. They were thirsty, and suffered dehydration and swollen tongues.

All the while, Worsley miraculously kept the boat on course. He had been able to take a navigational reading only the few times the sun had appeared through the clouds. On the morning of May 8, they had just spotted South Georgia when a hurricane tore through the area, "one of the worst hurricanes any of us had ever experienced," Shackleton said. It was clear they were being thrust onto the rocky crags of the island. The captain thought to himself, "What a pity. We have made this great boat journey and nobody will ever know."

When the wind shifted, the pin holding the mast broke. Mercifully it had lasted that long. "Just when things looked their worst, they changed for the best," Shackleton wrote in *South,* paraphrasing Browning's "Prospice."

They landed the boat the next day. They were safe though desperate for water and solid ground. Their voyage was a feat that nearly a century later is still hailed as the greatest boat journey ever accomplished.

The men heard babbling water and rushed to find a spring of fresh water. They fell to their knees to drink their fill. "It put new life into us," Shackleton said. "It was a splendid moment."

SHACKLETON'S WAY OF FORMING
GROUPS FOR THE TOUGHEST TASKS

- The best way to handle the biggest tasks is often to divide the staff into teams. Create units that are self-sufficient, but understand they won't all be equal. It is more important that the teams are balanced when considering the big picture.

- Make sure you have some cracker-jack groups that can handle the toughest challenges. They can also help others, to ensure no team falls far behind.

- Give the tedious assignments to the workhorses who don't complain. Let them know you are aware that you are giving them an outsized task and that you count on their good will and exceptional fortitude to get the job done.

- Empower the team leaders so they have the authority to handle their own group, but keep an eye on the details. Never let yourself be surprised by problems down the road.

- Don't be afraid to change your mind when you see your plan isn't working. You won't look indecisive if you show the logic of your changes.

- Be self-sacrificing. Give whatever perks it is in your power to dispense.

- Give a show of confidence in those acting in your stead. It's important that your support staff maintain in your absence the same level of competency you set.

- Never point out the weaknesses of individuals in front of others. Often, it's better to let everyone share in a remedy aimed at a few. Chances are, even the strongest will benefit from it.

WORKING IT IN

Capt. James A. Lovell Jr. has something in common with Shackleton, having been the leader of another famous "successful failure," as NASA dubbed the ill-fated *Apollo 13* flight. The 1970 mission never landed on the moon as planned, but with the benefit of level-headed leadership and teamwork it returned to Earth without any loss of life, overcoming nearly impossible odds.

"People like Shackleton and myself are individuals who can take on challenges—challenges that might include the unexpected," Capt. Lovell says. "You go in knowing everything is not going to work, and if you can think of things that can go wrong you can 'think ahead.'"

The astronaut reflected on his ordeal in space during a trip to the Antarctic in January 2000 to visit the National Science Foundation's station at the South Pole. Beforehand, Capt. Lovell had read about Shackleton and what he calls the "miraculous leadership" he showed in rescuing the crew of the *Endurance*.

"I think he took the same attitude we took on *Apollo 13*: You have to look forward as long as there is a chance," Capt. Lovell says of the Antarctic explorer.

Capt. Lovell was the same age as Shackleton, forty-two, when he, too, faced the toughest trial of his life. The astronauts on *Apollo 13* had just finished a television broadcast on the third day of their flight when an oxygen tank exploded as they turned on the heating system. The accident damaged the ship's fuel cells that provide electricity and support the propulsion system. Even worse, the command module started leaking oxygen into space. That led Capt. Lovell to utter those now-famous words: "Houston, we've had a problem." The crew, which also included John L. Swigert Jr. and Fred W. Haise Jr., was 200,000 miles from Earth and their safe return was uncertain, to say the least.

With just fifteen minutes of power left for the life-support systems, the men were forced to abandon ship for the tiny lunar module, beginning an intense four-day struggle to survive. The module was designed to sustain only two men for forty-five hours. The *Apollo 13* crew, under the direction of Mission Control in Houston, would have to turn it into a lifeboat that would accommodate three men for twice that time. The men were cramped and enormously uncomfortable. The temperature inside the module plunged to near freezing, making it hard to sleep. They had to drastically cut down on food and water, becoming severely dehydrated. Capt. Lovell dropped fourteen pounds during the ordeal. They improvised constantly, making adjustments to essential life-sustaining equipment with whatever sundry items were on board—cardboard, tape, plastic bags. At the most critical point, when the men had to set a course to prepare for the final push home, they couldn't see out of the debris-covered window to take a sextant reading. The bits of shattered Mylar that were hugging the craft shimmered in the sun, making it impossible to distinguish them from the stars. With a great deal of trouble, but amazing accuracy, they were able to adjust procedure to use the sun as a navigational star.

On April 17, 1970, almost fifty-four years to the day that the *Endurance* crew left their lifeboats and stepped onto Elephant Island, the *Apollo 13* crew climbed back into the command ship and powered it up for the perilous journey home. Hours later they splashed into the Pacific Ocean near Samoa. All were safe. Only a couple of secondary experiments and some photography were recovered from the mission.

Capt. Lovell gives credit for the rescue to the seamless teamwork between Mission Control's brilliant scientists and engineers who drew up detailed plans and instructions, and the well-trained astronauts who made them work. Shackleton and his men, of course, didn't have the benefit of outside help. Still, the captain sees a common thread in how people successfully survive a crisis. "I think it's very important that everybody has a job to do and everyone chips in," the former astronaut says. "In *Apollo 13* there was no panic, no one swore, we all just went to work on what went wrong and how to get this thing back."

In the direst circumstances, he believes people stick together and look to their leader for guidance. In such times, he adds, only one person can act as leader.

Capt. Lovell was the most experienced astronaut of his day, in terms of the number of hours logged in space. He was also among the most successful, helping to take space exploration forward in several respects. In 1965 he was the pilot of *Gemini 7*, which completed the first rendezvous of two manned spacecraft and set a record of fourteen days in space. The following year, he was commander of the last *Gemini* mission. *Gemini 12* linked with a satellite and Buzz Aldrin took a space walk that demonstrated how to successfully work with tools in space. On Christmas Eve 1968, Capt. Lovell was pilot and navigator on *Apollo 8*, man's first flight outside Earth's orbit and the first to orbit the moon. Millions were enthralled by a television broadcast during which that crew read from the Book of Genesis to a backdrop of pictures of the moon from space. *Apollo 13* was his fourth and last mission.

Capt. Lovell retired the year after the manned space program was halted in 1972, and launched a career in business. To help make the transition to the private sector, he earned a degree from Harvard Business School's Advanced Management Program, adding to a long list of degrees. His many awards include the Presidential Medal of Freedom, the French Legion of Honor, the NASA Exceptional Service Medal, and, like Shackleton, the National Geographic Society's Hubbard Medal. He told the story of his *Apollo 13* flight in a 1994 book, *Lost Moon,* cowritten by Jeff Kluger.

Today, Capt. Lovell is president of Lovell Communications, devoted to disseminating information about the U.S. space program. He also runs a restaurant in Illinois called Lovells of Lake Forest, with his son, Jay, as chef.

Capt. Lovell knows something of the restlessness Shackleton felt throughout his life to always want new challenges. It's an urge that grows stronger once the fear of crises is gone. "You have to look ahead; you can't look back or rest on your laurels," he says. "I keep looking for new ventures, new projects, and new goals."

7

OVERCOMING OBSTACLES
TO REACH A GOAL

How they survived I dare not imagine. Determination and willpower.

—Walter How, seaman, *Endurance*

Scott Polar Research Institute

PEAKS AND VALLEYS

Tom Crean, Ernest Shackleton, and Frank Worsley were barely recognizable when they arrived at the Stromness whaling station after an unprecedented thirty-six-hour struggle to cross the island of South Georgia. A whaler wept at the sight of them. It is hard to believe they are the same men in the second photo, taken five months later in Chile after they rescued their comrades on Elephant Island.

Courtesy of Neil Silverman

S HACKLETON MARVELED THAT THE TWO MEN LYING ON THE bottom of the *James Caird* at the end of the boat journey were the two most pessimistic members of the entire *Endurance* crew. The young John Vincent "had served on North Sea trawlers, and he should have been able to bear hardships better than McCarthy, who, not so strong, was always happy," Shackleton wrote in *South,* in a thinly veiled I-told-you-so. McNeish, the other perpetual naysayer, also lay prostrate in the boat.

The men were so exhausted upon landing at South Georgia on May 10 that they couldn't pull the *Caird* out of the water. Shackleton let the others sleep while he kept watch over the boat, which was being tossed about in the waves. Several times he had to rush into the freezing water to push the *Caird* off the rocks. Finally, he couldn't stay awake any longer and called Crean to relieve him. Everyone got up a few hours later and cut the topsides off the boat and took out any movable gear. At the next big wave they dragged her to the shore, losing the rudder in the process.

The men had landed in King Haakon Bay, on the opposite side of the island from their destination, the Stromness whaling station. They weren't up to another 150-mile boat journey to the eastern side, and also feared that if they tried, the strong currents would sweep them past the island completely. They would have to cross on foot. They found a large cave—its entrance protected by fifteen-foot icicles—and camped there for a few days to regain some strength. They had rations for ten days, but were low on fuel.

The next day, they made a fire using wood pulled from the boat and supplemented their rations with some young albatrosses. Crean did the cooking, but the smoke stung his eyes, already raw from exposure. Crean groaned all night from the pain, which meant Shackleton didn't sleep either. He administered eye drops to the protesting patient, like a "worried parent" trying to get his child comfortable enough to sleep, as Worsley described the scene.

On May 13, to the men's amazement, their rudder "with all the broad Atlantic to sail in and the coasts of two continents to search for a resting place, came bobbing back into our cove," as Shackleton described it. That bit of extraordinary luck enabled them to load up the boat a couple of days later and sail about nine miles across the bay to a safer area of the beach and a better departure point for the trek. The Boss decided to have McCarthy stay with Vincent and McNeish and prepared Crean and Worsley to accompany him on the trek. They turned over the boat to make a hut for the three left behind, calling it Peggotty Camp after the "poor but honest folk" in Dickens's *David Copperfield*.

Shackleton left McNeish officially in charge despite his condition because he was the most senior man. Again, Shackleton wrote a letter leaving clear instructions about what he wanted the men to do if he didn't return in a few days. They were to take the boat and sail around to the other side of the island and seek help at one of the whaling stations.

The Boss estimated it was thirty miles to Stromness whaling station, but that was as the crow flies. They would trudge much more than that over the following thirty-six hours. They would have to traverse mountains, glaciers, frozen streams and lakes, and a waterfall. No one had ever explored a path across the island, and the only map they had simply charted the coast.

At 2 A.M. Friday morning, May 19, the men got up under a cloudless sky and a full moon, had some hoosh, and set out with Shackleton in the lead. McNeish, as a gesture of solidarity, struggled to escort the team for the first couple of hundred yards, then could go no farther.

Shackleton, Worsley, and Crean went on—climbing twenty-five hundred feet above sea level. They saw the dangerous cliffs, glaciers, and plains before them buried in ice and covered by a fog rolling in from the sea. They roped themselves together for a modicum of safety and started to descend. It wasn't long, however, before they were forced to head back up the mountain to take an interior route. The island was just five miles across at that juncture, but the far coast was made up of sheer cliffs impossible to negotiate, and three bays lay between them and Stromness.

It was a heartbreaking journey. Three times the ragtag party reached the top of a ridge only to find some obstacle blocking their way down on the other side. When that happened they had to retrace their steps and attempt a new path, wasting hours and precious strength.

Disheartened, they wondered if after all they had been through, they would die so near the whaling station. Shackleton gave his companions some hot food. "Come on, boys," he called to them, never showing his frustration. He was determined that on the fourth climb up they were going to get down one way or another.

Shackleton decided to take extreme risks when his options narrowed.

The Boss had come to the bitter realization that the hardest part was to be the stretch just before the goal when they were physically and mentally at their lowest ebb. All through the ordeal, Shackleton had done his best to avoid injury. Now he knew he had to take some real risks.

With the sun setting and the air getting colder, the men had to get off the top of the ridge. There was only one way to get down the nine-hundred-foot slope quickly. Shackleton asked if the other two were game for a ride down. They gave the answer he wanted. They took the rope they had tied around themselves and coiled it into a makeshift sled, sitting one behind the other "in the fashion of youthful days," as Worsley described it. They shot down the mountainside screaming and hollering the whole way. In a couple of minutes they were at the bottom—exhilarated, frightened, and grateful to be safe.

Shackleton had them stop to eat at 6 P.M. They had left the remaining sleeping bags with the men back on the *James Caird,* and even at the lower altitude it was too cold to camp. They had no choice but to push on. A full moon lit their path through the soft snow until they reached four thousand feet above sea level. It was midnight. "Still we were following the light," Shackleton wrote.

After twenty-three hours of constant marching, they stopped once more for food before they headed down a slope to what they thought was Stromness Bay. They were mistaken. At the foot of the mountain they were shattered to realize they were trapped by cliffs and had to climb back up again.

With exhaustion setting in, Shackleton called a halt. While the others slept, he as usual remained awake and watchful. He feared that any sleep they got now would end up being permanent; so after five minutes, he woke up Crean and Worsley and told them they had been sleeping half an hour in an effort to get them to feel they were more rested than they were.

Shackleton had developed a reservoir of personal
strength that sustained him through the worst struggles.

Shackleton's inner and physical strength seemed almost superhuman at times. He drew inspiration from many sources: his faith, other people, the literature of great thinkers. Above all, he kept things in perspective. He pondered larger questions—about life, love, freedom, choice, and camaraderie—all of which sustained him in times of crisis.

Shackleton wrote in *South* that any retelling of the *Endurance* story would be "incomplete without a reference to a subject very near to our hearts." He tried to put into words the spiritual dimension of his feelings: "When I look back at those days I have no doubt that Providence guided us, not only across the snow fields, but across the storm-white sea that separated Elephant Island from our landing place on South Georgia. I know that during that long and racking march of thirty-six hours over the unnamed mountains and glaciers of South Georgia, it seemed to me often that we were four, not three. I said nothing to my companions on the point, but afterward Worsley said to me, 'Boss, I had a curious feeling on the march that there was another person with us.' Crean confessed to the same idea."

That passage in *South,* published in 1919, has launched countless Sunday sermons. Most pleasing to Shackleton, no doubt, would be that it also became the inspiration for a passage in one of the most celebrated poems of the twentieth century, T. S. Eliot's *The Waste Land.* Eliot wrote:

> *Who is the third who walks always beside you?*
> *When I count, there are only you and I together*
> *But when I look ahead up the white road*
> *There is always another one walking beside you.*
> *Gliding wrapt in a brown mantle, hooded*
> *I do not know whether a man or a woman*
> *—But who is that on the other side of you?*

Shackleton's spiritual musings quickly became the subject of controversy, much of it spurred by his own remarks. He was later quoted as saying he wrote and lectured about the fourth presence for "the old ladies" in the audience. Whether he mentioned the presence for the sake of little old ladies or denied it for the sake of the good old boys, no one will ever know for certain. Years later,

Worsley's widow, Jean, recalled one of her husband's last lectures on the Isle of Wight before he died in 1943. In that lecture he had referred to four men crossing South Georgia. After the lecture, Mrs. Worsley pointed out his error. He didn't realize he had said it. "Whatever will they think of me," he replied, adding, "I can't get it out of my mind."

Clearly, Shackleton's religious upbringing had a lasting impact on his life. As a young apprentice, he once told his parents that he could find no one but a "Negro sailor" with whom to discuss religion "except in controversy." He had decided early on that a ship wasn't a fit place for worship, and didn't hold services on his own ships. But he remained unself-conscious about invoking God's name, especially when in desperate straits.

The Boss was even known to end an evening of good times by singing hymns. He was, however, just as apt to quote a passage from Browning, Tennyson, Milton, Shakespeare, or Service. His morality was based on optimism and finding goodness in people and doing good things. His biographers, the Fishers, wrote about Shackleton and the religion controversy: "To strive and thrive, to fight on and hope ever, to play a great part in a world with a happy ending, were living motives for him."

On South Georgia, in the early morning hours of May 20, Shackleton turned, as he often did, to Browning. "The worst was turning to the best for us," he wrote. The men had spotted the "twisted wave-like formations" in the cliffs around Husvik Harbor, where Stromness sits. They were within sight of their destination.

The men congratulated each other by shaking hands all around. Still, these last steps were not going to be easy, not by a long shot. They stopped to have breakfast. Meals were no longer rewards, only sustenance. But this meal was punctuated with a startling sound: the 7 A.M. steam whistle calling the whalers to work. "Never had anyone of us heard sweeter music," Shackleton wrote in *South*. "It was a moment hard to describe. Pain and ache, boat journeys, marches, hunger, and fatigue seemed to belong to the limbo of forgotten things, and there remained only the perfect contentment of work accomplished."

The three faced another choice: to go down an icy slope or take a five-mile detour. The Boss again asked the others their opinion, knowing they would opt for the slope. At this point they abandoned everything but a single sledging ration, one biscuit each, a rope, and an adze. They had to make it down a wall of blue ice about five hundred feet high—the equivalent of a fifty-story building. They were thankful to have the improvised cleat shoes that McNeish had cobbled before they left Peggotty Camp. Somehow, they made it to the bottom.

They climbed up yet another slope to a flat plateau. Just one more ridge stood between them and the station. As the Boss led the way over the flat surface, he suddenly found himself knee-deep in water—and sinking. He flung himself down on his stomach and told the others to do the same to distribute their weight. They were on a snow-covered lake. They made their way across two hundred yards to the far shore.

At 1:30 P.M. they watched a little steamer entering the bay twenty-five hundred feet below. They saw small figures on the boats, the first men they had seen outside the *Endurance* crew since they had left South Georgia more than eighteen months before. Then they saw the station factory.

Shackleton shook his companions' hands in a gesture of congratulations.

Again they shook hands. It was a simple, personal gesture that heartened the men and gave the Boss a chance to show the pride and gratitude he felt for each individual's contribution. Shackleton explained in *South* that it was "a form of mutual congratulation that had seemed necessary on four other occasions" during the expedition: upon reaching Elephant Island, landing on South Georgia, making it to the ridge at the start of the island trek, and glimpsing the rocks of Husvik.

They weren't safe yet. They trudged down the middle of an icy stream, wet to their waists. It was about to get worse: They heard the soft roar of water and discovered they had to get down a twenty-five-foot waterfall. Worsley and Shackleton lowered Crean on a rope. Shackleton went next. Then Worsley, light and nimble, fastened the rope around a rock and shimmied down, leaving the rope behind.

They had made it! Their ordeal was over, though they were left with nothing but the soaking wet clothes on their backs. But they had made it! They felt a flood of emotions—relief, gratitude, joy—mixed with more profound thoughts of their greatness, their insignificance, and to what they owed this victory. Shackleton wrote an eloquent tribute to the moment, and the whole experience, in *South,* paraphrasing Robert Service's *The Call of the Wild:* "We had pierced the veneer of outside things. We had 'suffered, starved, and triumphed, groveled down yet grasped at glory, grown bigger in the bigness of the whole.' We had seen God in his splendors, read the text that Nature renders. We had reached the naked soul of man."

It was midafternoon on Saturday, May 20, 1916, when, shivering with cold, they approached the whaling station. "Our beards were long and our hair was matted. We were unwashed and the garments we had worn for a year without a change were tattered and stained."

Shackleton reported scaring two children and an old man who spotted them as they made their way to the wharf. There, they went up to the man in charge and asked to see the manager. The man asked who they were. "We have lost our ship and come over the island," the Boss replied. The man couldn't believe anyone could have walked across the island, and rushed to get the manager. When he emerged, Shackleton simply said: "My name is Shackleton."

They all knew who Shackleton was, but they certainly hadn't expected to see him there, and in that shape. A tough whaler later said, in broken English, "Me—I turn away and weep. I think manager weep, too."

Shackleton wrote that on the following night at dinner, the Norwegian whalers at the station, with no language in common, paid tribute to the men. They stood as every man walked silently up to them and shook their hands, each wanting to congratulate personally the men who had made the magnificent boat journey. After the *Nimrod* expedition, Shackleton had been knighted by the king and received medals from heads of state in every corner of the world. But for him, the greatest reward of all was this moment of quiet recognition from fellow seamen.

Shackleton's men were sustained
by the faith and trust they had in their leader.

Back on Elephant Island, it also seemed like a special time. Macklin wrote in his diary: "Yesterday and today have been two fine days. Yesterday especially the colors of sky and sea and glacier were wonderful, far surpassing anything I ever saw before. I will not make an attempt to describe this, for I could not possibly convey an accurate impression of these splendors. . . .

"This place can be very nice when it wants, but it generally prefers to act the devil."

Frank Wild had kept the twenty-one men under his care healthy, sane, and hopeful. Wild was the one person who had learned the art of leadership under the Boss's personal tutelage. In diaries kept by the *Endurance* crew, the men expressed their admiration for how well he was able to carry on during Shackleton's rescue mission. "It is not too much to claim that we owed our lives to his leadership," Hurley wrote after the crew's rescue. "He certainly justified the confidence Shackleton had placed in him."

Wild followed Shackleton's model to the letter: Soon after Shackleton had left for South Georgia, Wild had given a simple speech laying down ground rules. He addressed the party "concisely yet pertinently relative to future attitudes and routine," Hurley wrote the day after the *Caird* left.

Always, he set an example by being positive himself, regardless of what he might have been feeling. "He was unfailingly optimistic, and disapproved strongly if anyone showed a long face," Hurley explained.

Wild showed himself to be a tower of strength. He was the only one who didn't become listless, even when the crew had exhausted all but four days' worth of food. He had the men start every day by making preparations to leave the island, getting them out of their beds, and keeping alive their hopes of a rescue. Hussey said that Wild would yell out, "Roll up the sleeping bags, boys! Roll up your sleeping bags! The Boss may come today! And we want to be ready!"

He also staved off depression by keeping everyone busy. Early in the group's stay on Elephant Island, Macklin wrote, "I spent this morning the most unhappy hour of my life—all attempts seemed so hopeless, and Fate seemed absolutely determined to thwart us. Men sat and cursed not loudly but with an intenseness that showed their hatred of this island on which we had sought shelter. But the gloom lasted only a short time, however." After breakfast, Wild had put them to work finishing their shelter.

Wild made sure they had many everyday diversions. "We have something to read and, by exchanging, can always get a change," Macklin said. Five volumes of the *Britannica* had made it to the island, and one or two men kept their poetry books. But standards were slipping. Marston kept a small cookbook from which he read aloud one recipe every night. The men would comment on it and make suggestions on how to improve it. By that time they were fed up with meat and had mad cravings for energy-giving carbohydrates and sugar.

Wild also kept special celebrations going, especially the traditional Sweethearts and Wives toast every Saturday night. He allowed the men to concoct drinks using the alcohol supplied for the stoves mixed with some leftover ginger flavoring. It was barely tolerable, but it sufficed. The men used it to toast the second anniversary of their departure from England. The alcohol ran out shortly after that.

Wild took care of every detail concerning the individuals. Macklin mentioned that Wild once gave him a haircut and a shave so that he would feel more comfortable. More important, the second in command had learned from the Boss that careful preparation of the food was necessary for the men's mental and physical nourishment. Macklin wrote that for as long as possible the men "were fed 'full and plenty.'" A month after the Boss had left, he was more philosophical. "Destitute as we are—and we are certainly very destitute now—I think we are better off than many poor folk at home. We get plenty of meat and we are snug and warm in our shelter."

With the usual insistence on fairness that characterized the expedition, Wild distributed the food without complaint by using the "whose" method and by having the men rotate their seats at mealtimes so everyone had an equal chance to sit near the fire.

In all, the men were relatively happy. To their own amazement, they continued to find things to discuss. Only once during the long and anxious wait for a rescue did the words turn harsh enough to demand Wild's intervention. The argument was between Marston and Green and was about, of all things, ladies' hats. Green said his wife wore a hat of one shape, and Marston said his wife wore a hat of another shape, and each insisted his spouse was the more fashionable. They almost came to blows until Wild pointed out the absurdity.

One of the ways the men kept on an even keel was to write songs—often about each other. At the midwinter festival on June 22, after two months of enduring the grim conditions of the island, James scored the hit of the evening with a song entitled, "Our Hut on Elephant Isle," which paid tribute to Wild:

My name is Franky Wild-O, and my hut's on Elephant Isle
The most expert of Architects could hardly name its style
Yet as I sit inside, all snug and listen to the Gale
I think the pride is pardonable with which I tell my tale.

Chorus:

O Franky Wild-O tra-la-la-la-la-la

Mr. Franky Wild-O tra-la-la-la-la-la

My name is Franky Wild-O, my hut's on Elephant Isle,

The walls without a single brick, & the roof's without a tile

But nevertheless I must confess, by many and many a mile

It's the most palatial dwelling place, you'll find on Elephant Isle.

"If we are ever to be rescued we all heartily hope it won't be this day or at least not until after supper tonight," Orde-Lees wrote that day. It was this day that he described as "one of the happiest days of my life."

Shackleton's thoughts of his men
helped to spur him beyond his limits.

The Boss, of course, did not let his men down. As much as his men owed their lives to him, he also credited them with saving his. He often wondered if he would have made it had it not been for the responsibility of those under him. "It might have been different if we'd had only ourselves to think about," he wrote. "You can get so tired in the snow, particularly if you're hungry, that sleep seems just the best thing life has to give. And to sleep out there is to die, to die without any pain at all, like Keats's ideal of death. But if you're a leader, a fellow that other fellows look to, you've got to keep going. That was the thought, which sailed us through the hurricane and tugged us up and down those mountains."

Three days after Shackleton, Worsley, and Crean arrived at Stromness, they boarded a whaler, the *Southern Sky,* in a first attempt to rescue their comrades stranded on Elephant Island. They had to retreat six days later because of the thickening ice on the sea. Rather than return to South Georgia, they went to Port Stanley, Falkland Islands. There, Shackleton wrote letters to his wife and to an editor he had promised an exclusive, and cabled the king and Admiralty in London to plead for assistance in the rescue. He requested one of Scott's old ships, either the *Discovery* or the *Terra*

Nova, which were specially built for pack ice. The authorities were slow to respond, dealing as they were with the war. Even in peacetime, however, the soonest a ship could have gotten there would have been about two months.

McNeish, McCarthy, and Vincent were already on their way back to England from South Georgia. Within hours after he reached the whaling station, Worsley went to retrieve them from Peggoty Camp and Shackleton quickly arranged their passage to England. Sadly, McCarthy and another *Endurance* man, Alfred Cheetham, after surviving two years in the Antarctic, were killed in World War I.

Shackleton could be a stickler for protocol, but when bureaucratic delays jeopardized the safety of his crew back on Elephant Island, he acted independently, appealing to various South American governments for aid. On June 10, the government of Uruguay gave Shackleton the use of the *Instituto de Pesca No. 1.* That ship ran into heavy pack ice just twenty minutes from Elephant Island and was forced to retreat. In Punta Arenas, a group of local men underwrote the expenses of sending the wooden schooner *Emma,* which made it to within only a hundred miles of the island. The Admiralty by that time had agreed to send Scott's old ship, the *Discovery,* to the rescue, but it had to be repaired, suggesting long delays.

Shackleton wrote to Emily that he wanted to make one more rescue attempt immediately. The Chilean government gave Shackleton the use of the naval vessel *Yelcho.* Finally, with the worst of the winter past, the *Yelcho* left Punta Arenas on August 25. Five days later, on Wednesday, August 30, she reached Elephant Island.

Marston spotted the ship on the horizon around noon as he was preparing to draw some sketches, and shouted to the others. When no one responded, he went into the hut to tell them. Pandemonium set in as the men rushed to grab belongings, tearing through their hut walls in a dash to the shore. Soon, they saw the Boss climb from the ship and into a lifeboat headed toward them. Wild was so overcome with emotion at the sight of Shackleton he couldn't speak. The others tried to cheer but their voices, too, got stuck in their throats. The first words out of Shackleton's mouth were, "Are you all well?"

Everyone was. Thanks to Wild, well schooled in Shackletonian optimism and practicality, all the men had pulled through the five months of "the most nightmarish of nightmares," as Shackleton called their ordeal.

Shackleton, ever thoughtful, brought along the mail that had been collecting for the crew since they had sailed from the island. He also brought some newspapers, and the men were horrified to read that the war was still raging and the death toll was staggering.

On September 3, Shackleton sent a letter to Emily from Punta Arenas. "My Darling, I have done it," he crowed. "Not a life lost and we have been through Hell."

Shackleton, a master of publicity, told his men on the return voyage to Chile not to clean up too much. Crowds would be awaiting their arrival in Punta Arenas, and they would make more of an impact looking unkempt and wild. The ordeal was over for the *Endurance* crew— for everyone, that is, except Shackleton. He still had to rescue the men from the other half of the expedition on the Ross Sea.

Shackleton remained aware of the needs of the community.

The Boss must have desperately craved rest. He was deeply tired, depressed, and financially ruined. But in the midst of all his work to save his men—and far from the public eye or a camera lens—he performed a feat of remarkable selflessness. It was done on behalf of total strangers, it involved tedious tasks, and it came at a time when he was immersed in critical work. But Shackleton always kept sight of others in the world around him.

Today, Arthur C. Hall, ninety, of Tucson, Arizona, remembers the six weeks he spent with Shackleton and Worsley aboard a ship from South America in the autumn of 1916 and the kindness that was shown his mother and him.

Shackleton and Worsley were on board the *Parismina* making

their way to New Zealand to launch a rescue of the stranded Ross Sea party. The six-year-old Hall and his mother were bound for New Orleans from Valparaiso, Chile.

Mr. Hall's father had been an executive with a copper-smelting company and the young family had relocated to Chile in March 1916. Six months after their arrival, the senior Hall had contracted typhoid fever. He was taken to a hospital in Valparaiso from his home in Caldera but doctors there were unable to save him. The grieving mother was taking her son and the body of her husband home to California when they met the two explorers.

During the long trip, the odd foursome often shared a dining table. Mr. Hall remembers Worsley being the more talkative of the two men, telling the boy and his mother fantastic tales of exploration and survival. Shackleton, he recalls, was quieter, and "very, very thoughtful." The Halls had yet to pack up their South American home, so during a stop at Caldera, Shackleton, always the Boss, arranged to have the family's possessions packed up and brought on board. He also handled the family's weeklong stay at a hotel in Panama, guided them through customs in New Orleans, and made travel arrangements for the final leg of their journey home. The four shared a Pullman to San Jose, California.

After having just rescued twenty-seven people from disaster, and preparing to rescue others on the far side of the Antarctic, Shackleton took the time and energy to save two more people. Mr. Hall calls it "leadership in a quiet, efficient manner."

To this day, Mr. Hall cherishes a copy of *Ivanhoe* inscribed by Sir Ernest: "Arturo Hall, E. H. Shackleton on board *Parismina* Oct. 29, 1916." He says Shackleton also bought him a copy of *Swiss Family Robinson* in Lima.

**Shackleton worked
until the whole job was done.**

Shackleton then took on the task of rescuing the Ross Sea party, a team of ten men hired to lay supplies for the transantarctic crossing. While the *Endurance* stood trapped in the ice, the ship *Aurora* was also stuck, off the opposite coast of the continent. It had been blown out to sea before the men could land all their stores. After ten months of drifting in pack ice the ship was freed during a thaw and hobbled, damaged, back to New Zealand in March 1916. The survivors of the shore party were waiting for a relief ship to arrive.

In January 1917, Shackleton found seven of the ten had survived, though just barely. He wrote to his wife, Emily, that it seemed he was needed "personally all the time to be on the spot to clear and settle things." Capt. Macintosh, who Shackleton had placed in charge, had been overwhelmed by his duties. Shackleton wrote critically of his lack of organization but ultimately took responsibility himself for the loss of the men's lives.

Professor R. W. Richards of the rescued party was grateful that Shackleton had taken charge. "All of us who had not met him criticized him while we were in the Antarctic," he said. "You could see from the tone of my remarks what I think of him now. He was chock full of personality and a born leader—in my opinion the outstanding personality in all Antarctic exploration."

Shackleton finally returned to England in May 1917. By then, the fanfare that followed his reappearance in South Georgia had faded. The expedition continued to be controversial for its timing during the war, but many came to Shackleton's defense, calling his men courageous.

In his books and lectures, Shackleton offered this simple summation of the trials that his men on the *Endurance* had survived: "No words can do justice to their courage and their cheerfulness. To be brave cheerily, to be patient with a glad heart, to stand the agonies of thirst with laughter and song, to walk beside Death for months and never be sad—that's the spirit that makes courage worth having. I loved my men."

SHACKLETON'S WAY OF FINDING
THE DETERMINATION TO MOVE FORWARD

■ Go-for-broke risks become more acceptable as options narrow. Sometimes the potential rewards at the end of a daring venture justify the risk of suffering a spectacular failure.

■ Seek inspiration in enduring wisdom that has comforted or motivated you or others in times of crisis. It will get you through the most physically and emotionally draining times and help you to keep your perspective.

■ Congratulate yourself and others for a job well done. A pat on the back or a sincere handshake is an expression of personal thanks and gratitude that has never gone out of fashion.

■ Motivate your staff to be independent. If you have been a good leader, they will have the determination to succeed on their own.

■ Let your staff inspire you. At times, an overwhelming workload may force you to consider lowering your standards. Remember that the final product must represent the best efforts of the entire group.

■ Even in the most stressful situations, don't forget that you are part of a larger world that might benefit from your expertise. In turn, participating in community and family activities can give you skills useful on the job.

■ Make sure the whole job is done. Your staff may be able to call it quits after the heavy lifting is over, but you are responsible for seeing the work through to its successful completion.

WORKING IT IN

Michael H. Dale, retired president of Jaguar North America, has regarded Shackleton as a role model ever since he was a child in Birmingham, England, and learned about the explorer. Throughout his professional life, Mr. Dale has looked to Shackleton and various other historical figures for inspiration and guidance in matters of leadership.

He used Shackleton's example of focus and sheer determination to fire up a group of salespeople for a challenging campaign his company was launching to boost sales 50 percent over the following year. He told the story of the *Endurance* expedition at a meeting in January 1999 in Dubai, where most of the division's 139 independent dealers had gathered with Jaguar's sales force to discuss strategy.

"If you have the kind of commitment Shackleton had, you can absolutely achieve miracles" was the message he conveyed to the group.

What followed looked like a miracle. By the end of the year, annual sales of Jaguar cars surged to 35,039—a jump of more than 56 percent over 1998 figures. The division had finally beaten—and soundly—its previous sales record set in 1986 of 24,464 cars. "They were doing something right," Mr. Dale says of the dealers.

Of course, there are many reasons for Jaguar's improved performance, including the introduction of popular new models, a booming U.S. economy, and a worldwide trend toward premium brands. But Mr. Dale likes to give some credit to his speech. He says he got "tremendous feedback" from the audience and believes his comments inspired many employees to redouble their efforts to do their best. "The one thing Shackleton carried with him was his determination," he says. "While you breathe, there's still a chance."

Mr. Dale showed such determination himself when he became president of the division's Mahwah, New Jersey, headquarters in October 1990. Jaguar Ltd., of England, had just been sold to Ford Motor Co. for $2.5 billion, in a move many observers thought was a critical mistake. By 1994, Ford had reported more than $1 billion in operating losses and restructuring charges for the acquired company. Jaguar's North American division alone posted losses of more than $1 million a day for a two-year period.

The luxury-car boom of the 1980s had crashed by the early 1990s, but Jaguar was also being sharply criticized for its poor quality. "Overcoming the fear of ownership is our biggest marketing challenge in the U.S.," Mr. Dale said at the time.

Mr. Dale fought hard for the survival of Jaguar. In 1992, he cut the division's staff by nearly 40 percent and focused the remaining personnel on radically improving the company's reputation for customer satisfaction. Soon afterward, Jaguar began a steady roll-out of new models. Strong sales of the new XJ6 luxury sedan in the last quarter of 1994 led Jaguar to post its first profit since 1990. Sales continued to climb as the XK8 replaced the XJS in 1997 and the competitively priced S-Type was introduced in 1999. At the same time, Mr. Dale was helping bring dealers back to profitability and increasing Jaguar's visibility by expanding advertising to prime-time television.

His efforts were further rewarded in mid-1999 when Jaguar tied for first with Cadillac and Volvo in the sales satisfaction index for 1999-model cars in a nationwide survey conducted by J. D. Power & Associates of Agoura Hills, California. Mr. Dale, in a classically Shackletonian move, gave far-reaching credit for the achievement: "Every member of our team, from those on the factory floor to our employees here in the U.S. and our dealers throughout the country, played a key role in reaching this milestone."

More good news came the following year. Spurred by the success of the S-Type cars, U.S. sales in the first five months of 2000 already had increased 80 percent increase over all of 1999. On that note, Mr. Dale retired from Jaguar after forty-two years with the company.

He began his career in the auto industry in England in 1955 at the age of twenty, working on the retailing side. He joined the

British Motor Corporation's sales division in 1957, eventually working in Africa and Latin America as well. In 1966, he moved to the United States as sales manager for BMC. In 1970, after a series of acquisitions, he was given responsibility for sales at Jaguar, among other divisions. He worked to eliminate Jaguar's old system of independent distributor territories and established a stronger dealer network to better handle quality problems and customer satisfaction. Following the demise of the MG and Triumph model cars, he played a major role in the 1980s in restructuring the company to focus solely on Jaguar, as the United States was by then the company's biggest market. He was named senior vice president of sales and marketing in 1985.

After he became president of Jaguar North America, Mr. Dale realized what an important role business leaders play in setting a tone in their workplaces. "My body language, the way I acted, and the way I spoke influenced everything in the company," he says. "Something I got upset about in the morning was all across the U.S. by ten thirty."

Mr. Dale kept his own spirits up throughout his career by maintaining a balance between his work and his life outside the office. He has a wide range of interests, including owning and flying several vintage aircraft. A former member of the Royal Air Force, he is a director of the National War Plane Museum in Elmira, New York, and the Experimental Aircraft Association Foundation, among other organizations. He is also in the Road Racing Drivers Club and was named a 1973 Sports Car Club of America national class champion after winning a series of races in his Austin Healey Sprite. He has been known to test drive Jaguar cars built by the company's Group 44 racing team, formerly based in Virginia.

Mr. Dale sees Shackleton as a good study in optimism. "He never gave the slightest sign, no matter how bad things got, that he wasn't going to survive."

He adds, however, that he had the advantage of having a mother who "was Shackleton's equal" when it came to keeping a positive outlook despite many hardships, and she imbued in her son a can-do spirit. "She, like Shackleton, didn't have a negative bone in her body," he says.

For Mr. Dale that kind of spirit is what helps draw the line between real leadership and simple management. "Managed people are simply told what to do," he says. "People who are properly led are motivated to do whatever is necessary to get the job done in the finest possible way and don't need much instruction."

8

LEAVING A LEGACY

I have served with Scott, Shackleton and Mawson, and have met Nansen, Amundsen, Peary, Cook, and other explorers, and in my considered opinion, for all the best points of leadership, coolness in the face of danger, resource under difficulties, quickness in decisions, never-failing optimism, and the faculty of instilling the same into others, remarkable genius for organization, consideration for those under him, and obliteration of self, the palm must be given to Shackleton, a hero and a gentleman in very truth.

—Frank Wild, crew member, *Nimrod;*
second in command, *Endurance* and *Quest*

LEAVING A LEGACY

Shackleton died on January 5, 1922. Seven of the eight men from the *Endurance* crew who had signed on with the Boss for the *Quest* expedition gathered around his grave to pay tribute to their leader. From left, Frank Worsley, Frank Wild, James McIlroy, Charles Green, Thomas McLeod, Alexander Macklin, and A. J. Kerr.

$\mathcal{S}$ HACKLETON WAS PROUD OF WHAT HE HAD ACCOMPLISHED, despite his disappointment over failing to achieve his dream of crossing the Antarctic. From the time his ship was crushed by the ice, he had one goal: to get all his men home alive. He did just that, using nothing less than the sum of all he had learned in his more than twenty-five years of work at sea—bolstered by his faith and his unflagging optimism. "I have been the means under providence of carrying the biggest saving out of disaster that has ever been done in the polar regions North or South," Shackleton wrote to his wife shortly after his return to civilization.

Shackleton had a knack for being able to turn every opportunity into a means for advancement. In ordinary times, he no doubt would have quickly parlayed his spectacular rescue into a launching pad for another ambitious expedition. As it was, he was feted as a hero throughout South America, Australia, New Zealand, and the United States. He must have been anxious to take all the knowledge, energy, experience, and expertise he had used merely to survive and focus it toward an achievement that would bring reward to him and his country.

When he returned to England in the spring of 1917, however,

the war was still draining resources. Shackleton immediately went to work for the War Office. For the next two years, he lent his talents to the effort—first, traveling to South America to whip up support for the British cause, then to work on the transportation of troops and equipment in northern Russia.

In early 1920, Shackleton was able again to turn his attention toward polar exploration. A Dulwich schoolmate stepped forward to finance his expedition plans and Shackleton's old mentor, Hugh Robert Mill from the Royal Geographical Society, helped design its scientific program. After a year of planning, Shackleton launched the British Oceanographical and Sub-Antarctic Expedition. Its aim was to circumnavigate the Antarctic to chart its coastline, explore remote islands in the area, and carry out extensive marine research. Shackleton, always in the forefront of new technology, took along a seaplane.

In a remarkable show of loyalty and fortitude, eight *Endurance* colleagues joined the eighteen-member expedition crew: Second in Command Frank Wild, Capt. Frank Worsley, Dr. Alexander Macklin, Dr. James McIlroy, meteorologist Leonard Hussey, Engineer A. J. Kerr, Able Seaman Thomas McLeod, and the cook Charles Green. The *Quest* left England on September 18, 1921.

Shackleton seemed much older than his forty-seven years as his health had been failing for some time. In Rio, he suffered a heart attack but wouldn't let Macklin examine him. The Boss steadfastly refused to give in to his ailments and pushed forward with his plans.

The expedition seemed to be dogged by bad luck from the start. The ship had numerous structural problems and had to undergo extensive repairs in various ports along the way. On Christmas, the *Quest* got caught in a gale that held it in its grip for five days. The men were exhausted by the time they neared South Georgia. Despite his own fatigue, the Boss refused to let Macklin wake Capt. Worsley for his watch one night, telling him, "You boys are tired and need all the sleep you can get." Three days later, he wrote in his diary, "I grow old and tired but must always lead on."

The *Quest* pulled into Grytviken harbor in South Georgia on January 4, 1922. Shackleton was filled with nostalgia. He entertained the new crew members with stories of his remarkable boat journey and of how he had crossed the island on foot with his two companions. Happy to be back in his element, he wrote in his diary that night that it had been "a wonderful evening," and ended the day's entry with a simple line of poetry: "In the darkening twilight I saw a lone star hover, gem-like above the bay." Hours later, in the early morning of January 5, the Boss was dead of a heart attack.

Shackleton once summed up for a friend how he viewed life and leadership. "Some people say it is wrong to regard life as a game; I don't think so," he was quoted as saying. "Life to me means the greatest of all games. The danger lies in treating it as a trivial game, a game to be taken lightly, and a game in which the rules don't matter much. The rules matter a great deal. The game has to be played fairly, or it is no game at all. And even to win the game is not the chief end. The chief end is to win it honorably and splendidly. To this chief end several things are necessary. Loyalty is one. Discipline is another. Unselfishness is another. Courage is another. Optimism is another. And Chivalry is another."

Add to that list: intelligence. Shackleton's chivalry and charm may have opened doors for him in his lifetime, but decades after his death, the durability of his strategy rests on its timeless common sense and intelligence. Consider the examples this book offers of the people the Boss has inspired and impressed: a space explorer, a progressive military leader, a scientist, an innovative educator, an Internet pioneer, and corporate executives from the new economy, the service sector, and traditional manufacturing.

Shackleton was frustrated that he never got to write a book about "the mental side" of his leadership—what we would today call strategy. "That is the side, looking back, which interests me most," he said. Instead, he opted to write the ever-popular adventure tale. This book attempts to provide what Shackleton wished to explain about his experiences and achievements.

Ten years after Shackleton's death, the Royal Geographical Society installed a statue of him at its London headquarters. At the dedication ceremony, Lord Zetland, a major contributor to the project, predicted that in years to come, the explorer would be remembered primarily for his *Nimrod* expedition. It was, he reasoned, his greatest success in terms of discovery and new territory covered.

Time has proved otherwise. Leadership, after all, is more than just reaching a goal. It is about spurring others to achieve big things, and giving them the tools and the confidence to continue achieving. The Boss made all those under him see the full potential of their talents and had a lifelong impact on the men he led. "A Shackleton man remains a Shackleton man," said *Nimrod* geologist Raymond Priestley. He made the comment many years after Shackleton's death, despite the fact that he was better known for his work on Scott's *Terra Nova* expedition.

With Shackleton, of course, there was a very human side to his support of his men that lasted beyond their work together. Dr. James McIlroy told an interviewer that Shackleton was a constant visitor to his bedside when a combat wound confined him to a London hospital for fourteen months. When Seaman Walter How faced a financial crisis, Shackleton came to his aid, though he was rarely in the black himself.

He could never stop being a boss and protector. In June 1917, a month after he arrived home, Shackleton wrote a touching letter to Tom Crean encouraging him to do his best. It said: "Now about your own job, all I have been able to do is not much, for I am met with the statement that it is absolutely necessary for you to pass this easy examination before you can be considered eligible for the commission. You are sure to get it if you only do this. Why don't you buck up and tackle it? Go ahead old son. It means a lot to you. You say that the others are getting army commissions, they are not the same as the navy: the training is not difficult, a soldier is made in a few months, a sailor in years. You are not frightened of any seafaring job so don't let a little exam beat you."

Some months after Shackleton's death, seven of the eight *Endurance* crewmen who joined the *Quest* returned to South Georgia to pay tribute and have their picture taken at their leader's graveside. Emily Shackleton had asked that her husband be buried in the place he loved most, and he was laid to rest among the whalers' graves in the cemetery at Grytviken.

The *Endurance* crewmen had always been thankful that the Boss had saved their lives, but they also felt an indebtedness and a commitment that went further. "I am sure we are all the better for having known him and that his example to us made us see life as a bigger thing and not petty and small as some people see it," Hussey wrote.

Worsley added, "Something of his spirit must still live on with us."

Shackleton's legacy was his example of how to persevere against seemingly insurmountable odds. When he was asked by the headmaster of a boy's school what advice he might like to pass on, Shackleton told him: "The only message I can think of for your boys is: in trouble, danger, and disappointment never give up hope. The worst can always be got over."

Shackleton didn't live long enough to advise his own children on their futures. It is unlikely, however, that he would have either encouraged or discouraged his children to follow in his footsteps. Shackleton felt people should make their own journeys and their own choices in life. His youngest child, Edward, however, did keep alive his father's legacy by maintaining a lifelong interest in exploration, although his own experience in the field was limited. He received a medal from the Royal Geographical Society for becoming the first Westerner to climb Mount Mulu in Borneo in 1932, and two years later traveled to the Arctic region. Further showing he was a chip off the old block, he humorously described his Arctic destination as "a place young men went to cure their inferiority complexes and so learn how to talk to girls." Lord Shackleton, an author and a champion of many liberal causes, devoted most of his life to political service, rising to become Labor leader of the House of Lords. He died in 1994 at the age of eighty-three.

In 1999, Lawrence A. Palinkas, professor of family and preventive medicine at the University of California, San Diego, was asked to come up with a model for the ideal leader of astronauts working in long-term assignments in space. Dr. Palinkas is part of a NASA program that is training the Americans chosen to work in the sixteen-nation international space station, a $60 billion research facility more than two hundred miles above Earth that is scheduled to be completed by 2005. He needed to find someone who was successful at supporting teamwork, group living, and coping in a cramped and isolated environment for long periods

He thought of Shackleton. "Of all of the polar explorers, I admire him the most," says Dr. Palinkas, who has been to the Antarctic six times as part of his research on the psychosocial adaptation to extreme environments. "What impressed me about Shackleton was his flexibility—his willingness to admit defeat when necessary and to perform superhuman feats when necessary. I think flexibility, or adaptability, more than any other single trait, is essential to living in extreme and isolated environments."

Dr. Palinkas also admires the way Shackleton consistently motivated his crews and believes Shackleton's democratic style could combat one of the biggest problems for isolated groups: the tendency of members to fragment into cliques. "But it is his courage and this adaptability that enables Shackleton to transcend time and space as a leader," Dr. Palinkas adds. "With those qualities, he could be an ideal leader of a mission to Mars."

Perhaps the most important measure of a leader is the continuing relevance of his or her stature over time. Shackleton's legacy has not only endured but also broadened considerably. His popularity seems to have a resurgence at times when a general sense of contentment creates optimism and belief in human potential. At midcentury, amid many scientific and technological advances ahead of the space race, Shackleton emerged as the subject of at least two notable books: by Margery and James Fisher and by Alfred Lansing. Shackleton moved to the forefront again at the close of the century, when a booming economy brought leaps in technology and an enthusiasm for pioneering research.

Between those two periods, we can only imagine how many private challenges and special projects were inspired by Shackleton. His example covers many dimensions. In 1909, enjoying huge popularity, Shackleton became president of Browning Settlement, a club in London that offered education and recreation to men and boys from the poorest sections of the city. That first year, he was presented with the badge of the settlement, bearing his favorite line from "Prospice": "Sudden the worst turns the best to the brave." He remained the settlement's official head until 1917. Shackleton biographer H. R. Mill wrote that Shackleton preferred the club to his high-society haunts because "it was closer to reality and poetry." There, Mill explained, Shackleton "hailed the working men as brothers for, as he told them, he had been a worker ever since he shoveled coal at Iquique [Chile] on the deck of his first ship."

Shackleton's sense of duty to the community also makes him particularly relevant to today's executives: "His courage and determination can be a model for all of us, whatever occupations we have," says John C. Whitehead, who in 1999 joined actor and businessman/philanthropist Paul Newman to launch the Committee to Encourage Corporate Philanthropy, which asks CEOs to increase their companies' philanthropic giving. The committee's goal is to have total annual corporate giving in the United States expand 50 percent, to $15 billion, by 2004.

"I think determination is an important part of business success, maybe a more important part than is generally recognized," adds Mr. Whitehead, who in 1999 also became chairman of the newly formed Goldman Sachs Foundation. He worked thirty-seven years at Goldman Sachs, where he became cochairman and senior partner at the investment-banking firm.

Mr. Whitehead believes people in business can make valuable contributions outside the workplace because of their skill in making up budgets, setting goals and objectives, monitoring performance, getting hard work out of staffs, and raising money. Helping people and communities locally and globally is not an altruistic goal for corporate leaders, he says. "It makes things better for their employees and their customers, and that's a healthy result for business."

Jonathan Karpoff, University of Washington finance professor, believes the reason Ernest Shackleton is so compelling today isn't just that he survived against incredible odds but that he succeeded in the important things. "We long for the teamwork and camaraderie that the Boss inspired," he says. "We admire his ability to recognize both the faults and potential of his men, and his willingness to lead by example. We empathize with the loneliness that haunted his tough decisions. And we praise his understanding that respect for human life trumps any short-term prize. Ultimately, Shackleton is a success because, in him we catch glimpses of who we want to be."

Shackleton never planted a flag at the South Pole, he never made many of his goals, and he never earned all the money he wanted. Yet he was doing what he wanted to do, and he did it well enough to earn a place in history. His workplace was creative, productive, and enjoyable. He accomplished big things because he encouraged the full participation of every member of his team.

Shackleton is admired today because we want his energy, his optimism, his courage, his sense of camaraderie—and his unstoppable drive to push forward.

SHACKLETON'S THOUGHTS ON LEADERSHIP

- "There are lots of good things in the world, but I'm not sure that comradeship is not the best of them all—to know that you can do something big for another chap."

- "Optimism is true moral courage."

- "Leadership is a fine thing, but it has its penalties. And the greatest penalty is loneliness."

- "A man must shape himself to a new mark directly the old one goes to ground."

- "The loyalty of your men is a sacred trust you carry. It is something which must never be betrayed, something you must live up to."

- "I have often marveled at the thin line which separates success from failure."

- "You often have to hide from them not only the truth, but your feelings about the truth. You may know that the facts are dead against you, but you mustn't say so."

- "If you're a leader, a fellow that other fellows look to, you've got to keep going."

SHACKLETON'S CREWS

FIFTIETH REUNION

The surviving members of the *Endurance* expedition met in London in August 1964 for the fiftieth anniversary of their departure for the Antarctic. From left, Walter How, Charles Green, William Bakewell, Alexander Macklin, Lionel Greenstreet, and James McIlroy.

The *Endurance* Crew

Ernest H. Shackleton, Leader
Frank Wild, Second in Command
Frank Worsley, Captain
Lionel Greenstreet, First Officer
Hubert T. Hudson, Navigating Officer
Thomas Crean, Second Officer
Alfred Cheetham, Third Officer
Louis Rickinson, First Engineer
A. J. Kerr, Second Engineer
Alexander H. Macklin, Surgeon
James A. McIlroy, Surgeon
James M. Wordie, Geologist
Leonard D. A. Hussey, Meterologist
Reginald W. James, Physicist
Robert S. Clark, Biologist
James Francis (Frank) Hurley, Photographer and
    Cinematographer
George E. Marston, Artist
Thomas H. Orde-Lees, Storekeeper and Motor Expert
Harry McNeish, Carpenter
Charles J. Green, Cook
Walter How, Able Seaman
William Bakewell, Able Seaman
Timothy McCarthy, Able Seaman
Thomas McLeod, Able Seaman
John Vincent, Able Seaman
Ernest Holness, Fireman
William Stephenson, Fireman
Perce Blackborow, Steward

The *Nimrod* Crew (Shore Party)

Ernest H. Shackleton, Leader, Farthest South Party
Jameson Boyd Adams, Second in Command, member of
    Farthest South Party
T. W. Edgeworth David, Chief Scientist
Douglas Mawson, member of Scientific Staff
Raymond Priestley, Geologist
Eric Marshall, Surgeon and Cartographer, member of Farthest
    South Party
James MacKay, Biologist and Surgeon
James Murray, Biologist
Philip Brocklehurst, member of Shore Party
George E. Marston, Artist
Frank Wild, Sledger, member of Farthest South Party
Bernard Day, Motor Expert
Ernest Joyce, member of Shore Party
George Armytage, member of Shore Party
William Roberts, Cook

The *Quest* Crew

Ernest H. Shackleton, Leader

Frank Wild, Second in Command

Frank Worsley, Captain

Alexander H. Macklin, Surgeon and in Charge of Stores and
Equipment

James A. McIlroy, Surgeon

Leonard D. A. Hussey, Meteorologist

A. J. Kerr, Engineer

D. G. Jeffrey, Navigator

Charles R. Carr, Aviator

G. Vibert Douglas, Geologist

George Hubert Wilkins, Naturalist

Harold Watts, Wireless Operator

James Marr, Boy Scout

James Dell, Electrician and Boatswain

Thomas McLeod, Able Seaman

Charles Green, Cook

Christopher Naisbitt, Ship's Clerk

S. S. Young, Fireman

H. J. Argles, Trimmer

Norman Mooney, Boy Scout (returned home from Madeira)

Robert Bage, (returned home from Madeira)

A. Eriksen, Harpoon Expert (accompanied only to Rio)

BIBLIOGRAPHY

Books

Amundsen, Roald. *The South Pole*. London: John Murray, 1912.

Armitage, Albert B. *Two Years in the Antarctic*. London: Edward Arnold, 1905.

Back, June Debenham, ed. *The Quiet Land: The Antarctic Diaries of Frank Debenham*. London: Bluntisham Books, 1992.

Begbie, Harold. *Shackleton: A Memory*. London: Mills and Bacon, 1922.

Bernacchi, Louis C. *Saga of the* Discovery. London: Blackie and Son, 1938.

Bickel, Lennard. *In Search of Frank Hurley*. South Melbourne: Macmillan, 1980.

——. *Mawson's Will*. New York: Stein and Day, 1977.

——. *Shackleton's Forgotten Men*. New York: Adrenaline Classics, 2000.

Bruce, William S. *Polar Exploration*. New York: Henry Holt and Company, 1911.

Cherry-Garrard, Apsley. *The Worst Journey in the World: Antarctic 1910–1913,* 2 vols. London: Constable, 1922.

Cook, Dr. Frederick A. *Through the First Antarctic Night, 1898–1899*. New York: Doubleday & McClure Co., 1900.

Crossley, Louise, ed. *Trial by Ice: The Antarctic Journal of John King Davis*. Bluntisham Books, 1997.

Doorly, Charles S. *The Voyages of the* Morning. London: Smith, Elder & Co., 1916.

Dunnett, Harding McGregor. *Shackleton's Boat: The Story of the* James Caird. Benenden: Neville & Harding Ltd., 1996.

Eliot, T. S. *The Waste Land and Other Poems*. London: Faber & Faber, 1940.

Fisher, Margery and James. *Shackleton*. London: Barrie, 1957.

Fleming, Fergus. *Barrow's Boys*. London: Granta Books, 1998.

Fuchs, Sir Vivian. *The Crossing of Antarctica*. Boston: Little, Brown and Company, 1958.

Furlong, Nicholas. *Fr. John Murphy of Boolavogue, 1753–1798*. Dublin: Geography Publications, 1991.

Furse, Chris. *Elephant Island*. Shrewsbury: Anthony Nelson, 1979.

Gilles, Daniel. *Alone*. Boston: Sail, 1976.

Gordon, Andrew. *The Rules of the Game*. London: John Murray, 1996.

Gurney, Alan. *Below the Convergence: Voyages Toward Antarctica, 1699–1839*. New York: W. W. Norton, 1997.

Hattersley-Smith, Geoffrey, ed. *The Norwegian with Scott: Tryggve Gran's Antarctic Diary 1910–1913*. London: HMSO Books, 1984.

Hayes, J. Gordon. *Antarctica*. London: The Richards Press, 1928.

Huntford, Richard. *Scott & Amundsen*. New York: G. P. Putnam's Sons, 1980.

———. *Shackleton*. New York: Atheneum, 1986.

Hurley, Frank. *Argonauts of the South*. New York and London: G. P. Putnam's Sons, 1925.

Hussey, L. D. A. *South with Shackleton*. London: Sampson Low, 1949.

Joyce, E. M. *The South Polar Trail*. London: Duckworth, 1929.

King, H. G. R., ed. *The Wicked Mate: The Antarctic Diary of Victor Campbell*. Harleston: The Erskine Press, 1988.

Lansing, Alfred. *Endurance*. New York: McGraw Hill, 1959.

Lieder, Paul Robert; Lovett, Robert Morss; Root, Robert Kilburn, eds. *British Poetry and Prose*. rev. ed. Cambridge: The Riverside Press, 1938.

Marr, Scout (James W.). *Into the Frozen South*. London: Cassell, 1923.

Martin, Stephen. *A History of Antarctica*. Sydney: State Library of New South Wales Press, 1996.

Maslow, Abraham. *Eupsychian Management: A Journal*. Homewood: Richard D. Irwin, Inc. and The Dorsey Press, 1965.

Mawson, Douglas. *The Home of the Blizzard*. New York: St. Martin's Press, 1998.

Maxtone-Graham, John. *Safe Return Doubtful*. New York: Barnes & Noble Books, 1999.

Mill, Hugh Robert. *The Life of Sir Ernest Shackleton*. London: William Heinemann, 1923.

———. *The Siege of the South Pole*. London: Alston Rivers, 1905.

Mills, Leif. *Frank Wild*. Whitby North Yorkshire: Caedmon of Whitby, 1999.

Mountevans, Admiral Lord. *Adventurous Life*. London: Hutchinson, 1948.

———. *The Antarctic Challenged*. London: Staples Press, 1955.

———. *South with Scott*. London and Glasgow: Collins, n.d.

Murray, George, ed. *The Antarctic Manual*. London: Royal Geographical Society, 1901.

Murray, James, and Marston, George. *Antarctic Days*. London: Andrew Melrose, 1913.

National Science Foundation, Division of Polar Programs. *Survival in Antarctica*. Washington DC, 1984 Edition.

Ommanney, F. D. *South Latitude*. London: Longmans, Green and Co., 1938.

Priestley, Raymond. *Antarctic Adventure: Scott's Northern Party*. London: T. Fisher Unwin, 1914.

Pynchon, Thomas. *V.* New York: Perennial Classics, 1999.

Richards, R. W. *The Ross Sea Shore Party*. Cambridge: Scott Polar Research Institute, 1962.

Rubin, Jeff. *Antarctica*. Hawthorne: Lonely Planet, 1996.

Scott, Captain Robert Falcon. *The Voyage of the* Discovery, "New Edition," 2 vols. New York: Charles Scribner's Sons, 1905.

Service, Robert. *The Spell of the Yukon.* New York: Dodd, Mead & Company, 1941.

Shackleton, Sir Ernest. *The Heart of the Antarctic.* Philadelphia: J. B. Lippincott, 1909.

———. *South.* London: William Heinemann, 1919.

Shute, Nevil. *Slide Rule: The Autobiography of an Engineer.* London: William Heinemann, 1954.

Stewart, John, ed. *Antarctica: An Encyclopedia.* Jefferson NC and London: McFarland & Company, Inc., 1990.

Taylor. A. J. W. *Antarctic Psychology.* DSIR Bulletin no. 244. Wellington: Science Information Publishing Centre, 1987.

Taylor, Griffith. *Journeyman Taylor.* London: Robert Hale Limited, 1958.

———.*With Scott: The Silver Lining.* London: Smith, Elder and Co., 1916.

Wild, Commander Frank. *Shackleton's Last Voyage.* London: Cassell, 1923.

Wilson, Edward. *Diary of the* Discovery *Expedition.* New York: Humanities Press, 1967.

Worsley, Frank Arthur. *Endurance.* New York: Jonathan Cape and Harrison Smith, 1931.

———. *First Voyage in a Square-Rigged Ship.* London: Geoffrey Bles, 1938.

———. *Shackleton's Boat Journey.* London: The Folio Society, 1974.

———. *Shackleton's Boat Journey.* With a narrative introduction by Sir Edmund Hillary. New York: W. W. Norton, 1977.

Articles and Monographs

"A Brixham Man Who Shared Shackleton's Journey," *Herald Express,* October 6, 1960.

"About Lieutenant E. H. Shackleton," *Royal Magazine,* June 1909.

Dunsmore, James, "Shackleton of the S. S. *Flintshire,*" *The United Methodist,* May 4, 1922.

"England's Latest Hero," *Pearson's Weekly,* April 8, 1909.

Field, vol. 118, 1911

Hallock, Judith Lee, "Profile Thomas Crean," *Polar Record,* 22 (141),1985.

"Heart of the Antarctic," *Daily Telegraph,* November 4, 1909.

"Lieut. Shackleton's Homecoming," *The Daily Mirror,* June 14, 1909.

"Lieutenant Shackleton's Achievement," *Evening Telegraph,* (Dublin), March 24, 1909.

"Life on Elephant Island," *Buenos Aires Herald—Weekly Edition,* September 29, 1916.

Mill, Hugh Robert, "Ernest Henry Shackleton, M.V.O.," *Travel & Exploration,* Vol. ii. No. 7, July 1909.

Sarolea, Charles, "Sir Ernest Shackleton, A Study in Personality," *The Contemporary Review,* vol. 121, 1922.

Shackleton, E. H., "Lieutenant Shackleton's Own Story," *Pearson's Magazine,* September, October & November 1909.

"Speeches at the Unveiling of the Shackleton Memorial," *Geographical Journal,* Vol. lxxxix, No. 3, March 1932.

Diaries and Journals and Unpublished Papers

Clark, Robert S. Correspondence and papers. The Macklin Family.

Crean, Thomas. Correspondence with Captain R. F. Scott, Sir Ernest Shackleton, and Lady Emily Shackleton. The O'Brien Family.

Fisher, Margery and James. Correspondence and transcripts of taped interviews. Scott Polar Research Institute.

Greenstreet, Lionel. Correspondence. Scott Polar Research Institute.

How, Walter. Correspondence and papers. Scott Polar Research Institute.

Hull, George. Interview with Commander Lionel Greenstreet, August 24, 1974.

Hurley, Frank. Endurance *Diaries, 1914–1917*. Mitchell Library.

James, Reginald W. Endurance *Diaries, 1914–1916*. Scott Polar Research Institute.

———. Correspondence. Scott Polar Research Institute.

Macklin, Alexander H. Correspondence and papers. The Macklin Family.

———. Endurance *Diaries* and related papers, 1914–1916. The Macklin Family.

———. Quest *Diaries, 1921–1922*. The Macklin Family.

McIlroy, James A. Correspondence. Scott Polar Research Institute.

McNeish, Harry. Endurance *Diaries*. The Alexander Turnbull Library.

Miller, David. Taped interviews with colleagues of Frank Hurley.

Orde-Lees, Thomas H. Endurance *Diaries, 1914–1916*. The Alexander Turnbull Library.

———. Endurance *Diaries, 1914–1915*. Scott Polar Research Institute.

———. Endurance *Diaries, 1915–1916*. Dartmouth College.

Shackleton, Sir Ernest. Endurance *Diaries, 1914–1916*. Scott Polar Research Institute.

———. Correspondence and papers. Scott Polar Research Institute and Dulwich College.

Wild, Frank. *Sledging Diary* Nimrod *Expedition, 1908–1909*. Scott Polar Research Institute.

———. *Memoirs*. Mitchell Library.

Wilson, E. A. Correspondence with E. H. Shackleton. Scott Polar Research Institute.

Worsley, Frank. Endurance *Diaries, 1914–1917*. Scott Polar Research Institute.

ACKNOWLEDGMENTS

During the summer of 1969, I spent eight weeks at a camp in Vermont living in a small cabin with six other girls. This group seemed to click, almost magically, from the moment we met. About two weeks into the season, I walked into our cabin and was struck by a thought—for the remaining six weeks, would we continue to get along on such extraordinarily good terms? We didn't. But, for me, an interest in group dynamics was born.

In May 1984, I happened across a copy of *Shackleton's Boat Journey* in the Boston Public Library. Like many other people, before and since, I was fascinated by the story of twenty-eight men who lived cut off from the rest of the world, under life-threatening conditions, for almost two years and seemed to come through the experience pretty happily.

I wanted to know more than all the books I could find on the *Endurance* expedition told me. I wanted to know who was friends with whom; who was unpopular; who was hired in a management capacity and didn't live up to the role; who, on the other hand, was hired in a staff position and rose to take on additional responsibilities. I wanted to know what these men were really like; how they got along with each other, and what the secret was to their remarkable "unanimity." Eventually, I traveled halfway around the world to seek out the diaries from the expedition.

With no intention of doing so, I somehow was poked, pushed, and prodded by this compelling story to transcribe the diaries of two crew members, Thomas Orde-Lees and Frank Hurley. For my interests, the five-hundred-plus-page Orde-Lees diary was invaluable. He wrote on August 29, 1915, "I know that in reading all the other books on polar exploration nothing interests me more than the character of the leaders, but naturally one cannot always form a very concise opinion from the narrative written by the leader himself. I hope therefore that this impression of Sir Ernest by an intimate acquaintance will be of some interest to those who read it." It seemed as if he were speaking to me directly from the distance of eighty years.

In April 1998, Stephanie Capparell wrote an article for *The Wall Street Journal* about Sir Ernest Shackleton and his extraordinary *Endurance* expedition. The response on the part of the *Journal's* readers was tremendous.

In her article, Stephanie mentioned my years of research into Sir Ernest's leadership skills and by 9:00 A.M. the morning the article appeared, my phone was ringing with the first call from an editor asking if I would be interested in doing a book on the subject. Over the course of the following year I learned that killer whales, rogue waves, icy waterfalls, or—worst of all—twenty-one months trapped with twenty-seven co-workers are nothing in comparison to the daunting task of writing a book. Capt. Worsley's favorite epithet covers it: "Yoicks!"

In retrospect, it seems obvious that I should have called Stephanie immediately but in fact it took almost a year for us to meet and decide to work together on this book. Had I searched the world over, I couldn't have found a better coauthor. What a wonderful experience working with Stephanie has been.

Something I managed to do right, and a whole lot faster, through the generous guidance of Dava Sobel, was to find the perfect agent for this project, Michael Carlisle. Thank you, Michael, for a tremendous leap of faith.

I certainly had no idea that day in 1984 that one small book would end up taking me from Antarctica to Aberdeen and provide me with a host of friends on three continents.

I want to thank my friends in the Antarctic community for the many conversations that broadened my depth of knowledge on a wide range of matters Antarctic. The insights gained through conversations with Grant Avery, David McGonigal, Jeff Rubin, Judy Hallock, Harding Dunnett, Rob Stephenson, Shane Murphy, Joe Bugayer, and Martin Greene have found their way into this book.

Our thanks to Bob Headland and Philippa Smith at the Scott Polar Research Institute, Phil Cronenwett at Dartmouth College, Nigel Winser and Joanna Scadden at the Royal Geographical Society, Jan Piggott at Dulwich College, Valerie Mattingley at *National Geographic,* Stephen Martin at the Mitchell Library, David Retter at the Alexander Turnbull Library, and Adriana Abdenor.

Special thanks to Arthur Hall for sharing with us his memories of Sir Ernest and Frank Worsley.

For introducing us, we thank Caroline Alexander.

I thank Roland Huntford for a delightful afternoon spent discussing a wide range of subjects pertaining to Sir Ernest.

For her expert assistance with the manuscript, we thank Ellen Graham.

For being a mentor and role model, and for providing me with a living example of *Shackleton's Way,* I thank my dear friend, Judy Haberkorn.

At Penguin Putnam, we thank Clare Ferraro, Sarah Baker, Doug Grad, Louise Burke, Carolyn Nichols, Ivan Held, Paul Buckley, and Lucia Watson for sharing our vision of the book.

Stephanie and I want to thank the descendants of the *Endurance* men for providing a living and inspiring link to their fathers, grandfathers, uncles, and cousins.

In particular, we thank Alexandra Shackleton for expanding our knowledge of Sir Ernest through many introductions to family and friends. We thank Jeremy Larken for conversations on Sir Ernest's early career at sea and how those years shaped his leadership style and Peggy Shackleton Larken for perceptive comments on Sir Ernest's Quaker roots and Irish heritage and for her childhood impressions of her cousin. We thank Jonathan Shackleton for being a resource on the Shackleton family.

We thank the descendants of Tom Crean, Brendan and Gerard O'Brien, for memorable conversations and for making available the touching correspondence between their grandfather and Sir Ernest; and Hugh Crean for astute observations on the nineteenth-century Irish.

We thank Toni Hurley Mooy and Adelie Hurley whose zest for life and enthusiasm for adventure brought their father alive for us.

Most of all, I am enormously grateful to the Macklin family. In the 1950s, Dr. Alexander Macklin served as a unique resource for Shackleton's biographers, Margery and James Fisher, and for Alfred Lansing. Asking nothing more than that "the facts" be allowed to speak for themselves and that the story be told "without heroics," and with unparalleled generosity of time and spirit, Dr. Macklin answered letters and made himself and his papers available.

Two years before I met Dr. Macklin's sons, I had read the interviews that the Fishers conducted in the 1950s with surviving members of Shackleton's expeditions. Dr. Macklin's interview stood out. From the distance of forty years, Dr. Macklin's personality came shining through. He was funny, full of insights into the personalities of his comrades, had a wonderful memory and, above all, was forthright and fair. No wonder Sir Ernest hired him on the spot.

For opening their hearts, homes, and treasure trove of Shackleton material, I will be forever grateful to Sandy and Richard Macklin.

And lastly, I want to thank my own dear old Pa for always, always being there.

—Margot Morrell

I would like to thank my twin, Susan Cotter, for introducing me to the Shackleton tale; my editor at *The Wall Street Journal*, Mike Miller, who saw potential in an unconventional business story; my coauthor, Margot Morrell, for inviting me to join her on this project; my nephew, Michael DiCuccio, for assisting with the technology of book writing and with research on the space program; and my friends and neighbors in Astoria, New York, whose many generous acts were a huge help.

—Stephanie Capparell

INDEX

Note to reader: Illustrations are listed in boldface.

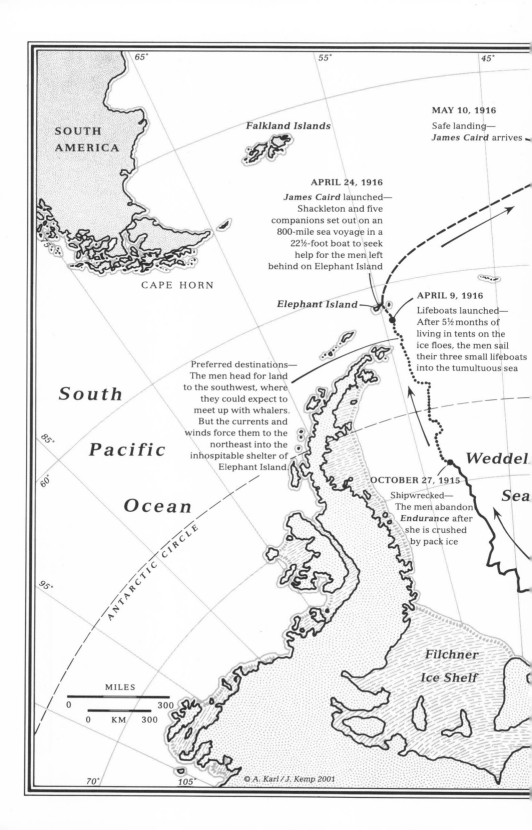

65° 55° 45°

SOUTH
AMERICA

Falkland Islands

MAY 10, 1916
Safe landing—
James Caird arrives

APRIL 24, 1916
James Caird launched—
Shackleton and five
companions set out on an
800-mile sea voyage in a
22½-foot boat to seek
help for the men left
behind on Elephant Island

CAPE HORN

Elephant Island

APRIL 9, 1916
Lifeboats launched—
After 5½ months of
living in tents on the
ice floes, the men sail
their three small lifeboats
into the tumultuous sea

South

Preferred destinations—
The men head for land
to the southwest, where
they could expect to
meet up with whalers.
But the currents and
winds force them to the
northeast into the
inhospitable shelter of
Elephant Island.

Pacific

85°

60°

Weddel

OCTOBER 27, 1915
Shipwrecked—
The men abandon
Endurance after
she is crushed
by pack ice

Sea

Ocean

ANTARCTIC CIRCLE

95°

*Filchner
Ice Shelf*

MILES
0   300
0   KM   300

70°   105°   © A. Karl / J. Kemp 2001